Hazlitt
in LOVE

Hazlitt
in LOVE

a fatal attachment

Jon Cook

✱ SHORT BOOKS

First published in 2007 by
Short Books
3A Exmouth House
Pine Street, London EC1R OJH

10 9 8 7 6 5 4 3 2 1

A CIP catalogue record for this book
is available from the British Library.

ISBN 978-1-904977-40-7
Printed in Great Britain by Mackays of Chatham, Kent

CONTENTS

INTRODUCTION

This story began as a piece of scandalous gossip in early nineteenth-century literary London. Its subject was a middle-aged man who had fallen in love with a woman half his age. It took on new life in 1823 when one of the two people involved in the affair, the writer William Hazlitt, published a book based on his passion. The book was called *Liber Amoris*, and its effect was to add further fuel to the scandal. For a number of years after the book's publication, the story had a muted existence until it was told again, later in the nineteenth century, as an episode in the memoirs of various people who had known Hazlitt or were related to him. And after that it became a major episode in twentieth-century biographies of Hazlitt. The story has been told in fictional form as well by Anne

Haverty in her novel, *The Far Side of a Kiss,* and, more obliquely, in Jonathan Bate's *The Cure for Love*.

Scandalous affairs invite judgements. Some have seen Hazlitt as the victim of his own mad passion, or of a young woman's calculating sexual curiosity. Others have seen him as a sexual predator intent on pursuing an innocent young woman who made clear that she had no special attraction to him. The situation was further complicated by the fact that Hazlitt wrote about his passion and published what he wrote. This had unpredictable and sometimes damaging consequences for him and for Sarah Walker, the woman he was convinced was the love of his life.

This book is perhaps inevitably swayed by this tradition of judgement and the need to find a villain and a victim in stories about sexual passion. However, its purpose is not to attack or defend, but to understand what happened. Central to this understanding is the fact that Hazlitt was a writer whose experience was deeply informed by his reading. Love for him was a passion, but the passion was fuelled by the tissue of quotations, stories and analogies that were part of the furniture of his mind. He was also a person who had a considered view about writers and love, one that only added to his intense self-consciousness about whether he was someone who would ever find the love he apparently craved. So being in love was part of a continuum that included reading and writing about it. There may seem nothing very unusual in that, but, in Hazlitt's case, it reached a peculiarly intense pitch of invention and reinvention. Love was not simply experienced in his meetings with Sarah Walker or in his hope that they might marry. A part of his being in love with her was what he actually wrote about her. Writing fed his imagination of what it meant to be in love. It was the medium in which he expressed and questioned his feelings.

Sarah Walker can too readily be seen as the opposite of Hazlitt, or his inferior. Her self-consciousness was different to his, not just because of her class and gender but because she didn't use writing as a means of self-expression or analysis. She left no record of what she felt about him. We can hear an echo of her words and an indication of her feelings in what Hazlitt wrote about her. She was certainly a screen on which he projected his fantasies of happiness and torment. She was curious about him and a part of that curiosity was sexual. But she also very clearly had an existence apart from him, one that we can glimpse in between the lines of his own writing about her. It is, of course, difficult to write biographically about someone who survives largely in the words of others. But, whatever may be true or not true about her, Sarah Walker seems to have had a degree of independence – one that her family acknowledged – that makes her something other than the victim of Hazlitt's desires.

Hazlitt's passion for Sarah Walker started in a lodging house in London, and led him to the divorce courts of Edinburgh. It also led him into a world of parallel stories and analogies. Like others before and since, he experienced love as a unique and unprecedented event in his life and then found himself living out a narrative that had been told many times before and one that had happened to many others. The time in which he lived was one that inherited and created some powerful love stories. In 1748 Samuel Richardson had published a European bestseller, *Clarissa*. In 1761 Rousseau repeated Richardson's success with another love story, *La Nouvelle Heloise*. In 1774 Goethe published *The Sorrows of Young Werther*. Hazlitt had read all these books. They affected the way he thought about love, but they had also become part of a much wider cultural atmosphere. For all their differences, these books shared some things in common. Their stories turned on a woman's refusal of courtship or seduction. This refusal could be uncompromising, as in the case of Clarissa; or it could be regretful and equivocal, as in the case of Julie in

Rousseau's novel; or it could be done out of devotion to another, as in the case of Lotte in Goethe's story. But in each case the consequences were the same: the death of one or both of the lovers. The old alliance between love and death was renewed in novels set in a recognisably modern world with modern characters.

There was also something else these books shared in common. They were all written in the form of letters. The main characters wrote about what they had done or what had been done to them. They examined their motives and passions. These novels, and others like them, not only told love stories, they also debated the nature of love. Was it an illusion? Was it just an idealised name for lust? Was it a ruse whereby one person gained control over another? Or was it the most valuable event in a human life? There was a great curiosity amongst readers about these questions. They were part of a cultural fascination with love that was very much alive during Hazlitt's lifetime.

Jane Austen, a contemporary of Hazlitt's, published her novels after the work of Richardson, Rousseau and Goethe. Her stories weren't told through an exchange of letters and they provided an alternative to tales of love and death. In *Pride and Prejudice,* Elizabeth Bennet refuses D'Arcy's marriage proposal, but is then given time to reconsider and agree to what she once refused without any loss in her dignity. Suicide, madness, the consummation of love in death, are all avoided in the name of a more benign and comic outcome. In Austen's world, love can be reconciled with social conventions. Attraction, intimacy, lovers' vows are not at odds with the world, but an important part of it.

Love stories are a part of love lives. They nourish the way that people imagine what love is and what its consequences might be. William Hazlitt and Sarah Walker lived in a culture that told itself rival stories about love. In one, authentic passion could not be reconciled with ordinary life. In the other, it could. Perhaps both were true. It was as though for both of them the truth of either story had to be tested.

CHAPTER ONE
LOVE AT FIRST SIGHT

On August 13th, 1820, 42-year-old William Hazlitt —
a well-known journalist, lecturer and political
radical — moved into two rooms on the second floor of a
lodging house at 9 Southampton Buildings, in Holborn,
London. Three days later, he met nineteen-year-old Sarah
Walker, his new landlady's daughter.

Hazlitt paid to have his breakfast brought to his room
on a tray, and on the 16th it was Sarah's turn to perform
this task. Her first appearance in Hazlitt's room met with
a mild compliment from him about her dress and manner.
But it was something about the way she left the room that
day that was to transform his life:

…the first time I ever saw you, as you went out of the room, you turned full round at the door, with that inimitable grace with which you do everything, and fixed your eyes full upon me, as much as to say, 'Is he caught?'…

There is no record of what Sarah felt about Hazlitt or saw in him at this first meeting. Contemporary portraits show a striking man, with long dark hair and an intense, pale face. He was physically agile and alert and enjoyed playing a strenuous racquet game called 'fives'. But his friend P.G. Patmore, who was to play an important role in his love affair with Sarah, remembered him sitting 'silent and motionless over his breakfast things till 7 or 8 o'clock at night from pure incapacity to take the trouble of moving off his chair and putting on his shoes to go out'. Patmore also remembered his social awkwardness. He had a 'strange and ungainly manner' and was often suspicious of other people: 'Hazlitt entered a room as if he had been brought back to it in custody'. John Clare thought him 'a silent picture of severity' when he met him in 1822 and, like Patmore, noticed his suspicious manner, 'throwing under gazes round at every corner as if he smelt a dun'.

In Patmore's account, Hazlitt was self-conscious,

intellectually intense and impatient with social conventions. He often imagined himself in love and would confide in his friends 'affairs of the heart' which usually turned out to be more imaginary than real. He lived on his nerves in ways that made his behaviour unpredictable. If he struck some observers as 'strange' – a word that Hazlitt seemed to attract – he also impressed the same observers with his intellectual power. The *Times* journalist, Henry Crabb Robinson, told his sister that he thought Hazlitt the cleverest person he knew. Patmore believed many of the people who disliked Hazlitt were envious of his originality and intelligence.

There are few accounts of Sarah's appearance, apart from what Hazlitt wrote about her; and, over the course of their meetings with one another, he was to see her in many different and contradictory ways.

One of Hazlitt's acquaintances, the playwright and journalist Barry Procter, recalled her in his memoir: 'Her face was round and small, and her eyes were motionless, glassy and without any speculation (apparently) in them.' Something in the way she moved impressed him: 'Her movements in walking were very remarkable, for I never observed her make a step. She went onwards in a sort of wavy, sinuous manner, like the movement of a snake.'

Procter thought her quietly spoken and reticent, although this may simply have been the way she behaved in the company of strangers.

If Hazlitt's account is to be trusted, Sarah and he rapidly became intimate. Bringing in the breakfast tray became an alibi. Sarah would stay in Hazlitt's room, sit on his knee, and let him embrace her. They would talk, or, as is more likely, she would listen to Hazlitt's amorous recitals. She fended him off when he threatened to become too physical. But, according to Hazlitt, Sarah was a willing partner:

> ...you come up here, and stay as long as I like... you sit on my knee and put your arms round my neck, and feed me with kisses, and let me take other liberties with you...

In the early weeks of the meetings he asked her to go to bed with him. She told him that she couldn't because she slept with her younger sister Betsey, who might tell her parents if her older sister was not with her each night. Hazlitt didn't put any more pressure on her. At the time it probably seemed a promising and temporary rebuff.

Either way he soon absorbed his first encounter with

Sarah into an elaborate Romantic mythology of love. He described her as a 'sweet apparition', a 'vision of love', and felt in his hopeful moods that she was the promise of happiness made flesh. He embroidered her with quotations and images. Sarah, he believed, possessed the grace of a Shakespearian heroine and the beauty of a Madonna by Raphael. She was sweet-tempered and kind in a way that Hazlitt believed only a woman could be. Her impact on him confirmed what he believed about the reality of love at first sight:

> I do not think that what is called Love at first sight is so great an absurdity as it is sometimes imagined to be. We generally make up our minds beforehand to the sort of person we should like, grave or gay, black, brown, or fair; with golden tresses or with raven locks; and when we meet with a complete example of the qualities we admire the bargain is soon struck. We have never seen any thing to come up to our newly discovered goddess before, but she is what we have been all our lives looking for. The idol we fall down and worship is an image familiar to our minds.

Sarah was to be his 'newly discovered goddess', his dream come true, and it was a dream that in 1820 Hazlitt needed.

***

Hazlitt's affair with Sarah Walker led him to divorce his wife and to gamble recklessly with his reputation, inspiring the most controversial book of his career, the *Liber Amoris*, or the *Book of Love* which he finally published about her in 1823. At first reading, the book is an astonishing piece of confessional literature, in which Hazlitt lays bare his inner life. He does this with enough power to shock and disturb a modern reader, who may find it both humiliating and repugnant. Indeed it might easily be dismissed as a brutal story of the sexual harassment of a working-class girl by a perverse, middle-class intellectual.

But Hazlitt's gamble was that his passion and honesty would ultimately win the sympathy of discerning readers. If this amounted to a display of Romantic egotism, then that was a risk he was prepared to take. What he had written about Rousseau could apply to his own work: '...it was the excess of his egotism and his utter blindness to everything else, that found a corresponding sympathy in the conscious feelings of every human breast.'

If, in these early meetings, Sarah transfigured the world for Hazlitt, it is unlikely that he did the same for her. He was one amongst a number of lodgers she had to look after; he was much older than her, and a married man. The demands of respectability worked upon them differently. Hazlitt's passion veered between respecting her virtue and wanting to satisfy his sexual desire. Sarah dealt with this by reminding him of her obligations to her family. If she had first rebuffed him by talking about the practical difficulty of their sleeping together, she rapidly added another line of defence. Her statement, in Hazlitt's recollection, was firmly poised: '...however she might agree to her own ruin, she would never consent to bring disgrace upon her family.'

These differences were compounded by others. Her appearance with a breakfast tray in his living room might encourage dreams in him of domestic bliss. But 9 Southampton Buildings was, for her, not a set of comfortable, quiet lodgings at fourteen shillings a week. It was the place where her family lived and worked. Her father, Miciah, a taylor, worked in the house. His wife Martha managed the lodging house. And then there was the rest of Sarah's family: her brother Miciah, nicknamed Cajah, her sisters Betsey and Emma, and a baby brother, John. Once able to, they would all be expected to help around the house. Sarah's duties were not exceptional.

The family occupied the ground floor of the building, where there was the kitchen, a living room, and a hallway. Above were two floors of corridors, staircases and rooms occupied by lodgers. Here actions could be seen or over-seen, conversations heard or overheard. At the time that Hazlitt first came to Southampton Buildings there were already three other lodgers installed: a married couple, the Follets, and a young Welsh apothecary called Griffiths, who lived in a garret room on the floor above Hazlitt's suite of rooms. Each had their own arrangements with the Walkers but most required some kind of service from Sarah. Mrs. Walker was clearly keen that her business should thrive.

From this point of view, her teenage daughter was a valuable asset, an attractive addition to the service provided for their main clientele: single men studying for or practising one of the professions or respectable trades. Sarah's guarded responses to Hazlitt's advances show the contradictory expectation of her family, at once respectable Dissenters but equally intent on making the family business profitable. Sarah had to keep the customers sweet whilst still preserving her reputation as a marriageable young woman. Certainly, in her parents' minds, the lodging house was a place where she might meet an eligible suitor. In 1819, her elder sister Martha had married a young lawyer, Robert Roscoe, whom she had first met when Roscoe was a lodger in Southampton Buildings.

Hazlitt met Sarah at a time of considerable difficulty in his life which may help to explain her impact on him. His fragile marriage had broken down about six months before their first meeting. In December 1819, his family had been evicted from their house on York Street, Westminster. Hazlitt had not kept up with the rent and for his wife Sarah this seemed a further – and this time, intolerable – episode in a long history of her husband's hopeless way with money. She took their son William with her to a cottage owned by her family in Wiltshire.

The disintegration of Hazlitt's marriage was followed in July 1820 by the death of his father, a Dissenting minister. His father's stoicism had become a point of stability and security against which his son had come to measure his own vulnerability to the world. Hazlitt had lost the reassurance his father's image gave him at a time when his reputation as a writer was becoming a source of seemingly inexhaustible and painful controversy.

The controversy had been gathering force for a number of years. Hazlitt was a radical who did not keep quiet about his political opinions. His early upbringing in Unitarianism and Dissent had encouraged him to question authority and delight in dispute and reasoned argument. From the age of thirteen to eighteen, he had been educated at Hackney College in London. During his time there the college became notorious as a hotbed for revolutionary ideas and sympathies.

The young Hazlitt was rapidly caught up in the excitement and the controversy provoked by the French Revolution, and had no doubt about which side he was on. 'I started in life with the French Revolution', he wrote in a nostalgic essay published in 1827, adding ruefully 'I have lived, alas! to see the end of it... My sun rose with the first dawn of liberty, and I did not think how soon both must set.' He thought the time in which he lived was dominated by a great struggle between liberty and tyranny, and he came to feel increasingly that the supporters of liberty were on the losing side.

The conservative side in the 1790s was represented by Edmund Burke, a writer whom Hazlitt admired, who in 1790 published an eloquent attack on the French

Revolution, *Reflections on The Revolution in France.* This drew a vigorous response from the radicals, most particularly Tom Paine's *The Rights of Man*, which echoed the French National Assembly's 1789 *Declaration of the Rights of Man* with its resounding first Article:

> Men are born and remain free and equal in rights.
> Social distinctions may be founded only upon the
> general good.

The implications of these assertions of the rights of man were rapidly taken up. In 1792, Mary Wollstonecraft, a founding figure of modern feminism, published her *Vindication of the Rights of Woman.* As the political order was changing, so, too, were assumptions about how men and women were to live together.

These arguments about the most basic questions in politics – what did it mean to live in freedom? What was the nature of a just and orderly society? What was the source of legitimate political authority? – were conducted in a charged atmosphere. England was at war with France and would remain so almost continuously until 1815. Government fears that the revolution in France might be repeated in England led to laws restricting freedom of expression and association. Back in the middle of the eighteenth century, the French philosopher, Voltaire, had thought Britain more advanced than any other country in Europe in its defence of individual liberty and its restraint of despotic power. By the 1790s that reputation was changing fast.

A combination of political risk and personal vitriol marked the journalism of the period, especially for those on the radical side of the argument. William Hone, who published Hazlitt's *Political Essays* in 1819, was the subject of a show-trial in 1817. Hone was charged with blasphemy, but the real motive for his trial was political rather than religious. The government feared that Hone would stir up seditious ideas amongst the poor. In the event he managed to persuade the jury that the charges against him were mistaken. He was acquitted amidst great public celebrations. John and Leigh Hunt, Hazlitt's colleagues and editors of the *Examiner*, a paper he wrote for regularly, were less lucky. In 1813 they were sentenced to two years in jail for libelling the Prince Regent.

It was in this atmosphere that, after a failed attempt to be a portrait painter, Hazlitt started his career as a journalist in 1812, reporting parliamentary speeches for the *Morning Chronicle*. In the same year he also gave his first series of public lectures on the history of English philosophy. He rapidly expanded the range of his writing. The next year he started writing short essays and drama reviews for the *Morning Chronicle*. In 1814 he left the paper after disagreements with its editor James Perry, and started to write for a number of liberal newspapers and reviews, and by 1817 he was publishing books based on his journalism and lectures.

Hazlitt's energetic style and political convictions made him a notable presence in the literary and political culture of his time. He was rapidly identified as a leading radical voice and this made him a target for his political opponents. In August 1818, the Edinburgh-based *Blackwood's Magazine* published an attack on him called 'Hazlitt Cross-Questioned' which soon became notorious. The article took the form of a set of questions intended to mock Hazlitt's character and style as a writer. They described him as 'wild black-bill Hazlitt' and dismissed him as an 'impudent charlatan', 'a mere quack... one of the sort that lounges in third-rate bookshops, and writes third-rate books'.

The intent of the editors of *Blackwood's* was clear and it was similar to the personalised campaigns of modern tabloid journalism. They wanted to destroy Hazlitt's career, attack the radicalism that he represented and taint, by association, the reputation of one of their commercial rivals, the successful Edinburgh publisher, Archibald Constable, who admired and supported Hazlitt's work. They employed a young spy, Alexander Henderson, who came to London, met Hazlitt, and relayed gossip about him back to the magazine's editors.

The attack certainly had an impact. His publishers, Taylor and Hessey, withdrew an offer of £200 for a book based on a lecture series he had given on *The English Comic Writers*. Hazlitt sued *Blackwood's* and, after some legal wrangling, settled out of court for damages of £100. *Blackwood's* subdued their attacks on Hazlitt for a while, but what they had started, others soon took up.

The publication in 1819 of Hazlitt's *Political Essays* gave renewed visibility to his radicalism. To some of his conservative opponents, Hazlitt was a fellow traveller with Britain's recently defeated enemy, France. But it wasn't just Hazlitt's political beliefs that made him a controversial figure. His style was attacked because it put his personal convictions, experiences and thoughts so much on display. He wrote, so his enemies claimed, to show off.

In November 1819, the *Quarterly Review* condemned his writing as the manifestation of a 'ludicrous egotism' and suggested that his political radicalism was a sign of madness. In the same year the *British Review* claimed that he was one of a 'class of writers, whose aim is to destroy the very foundations of modesty and decorum'. *Blackwood's* added an element of class condescension to these attacks. Hazlitt was a leading figure in what they labelled the 'Cockney School of Writers'. He was the 'Cockney Aristotle' to a 'Cockney School of Poets' that included John Keats and Leigh Hunt. According to *Blackwood's* and journals that followed in their wake, The Cockney School was a group of literary upstarts. Their style was an abuse of proper English, their politics an abuse of the English constitution, and their fascination with erotic imaginings, typified by poems like Keat's *Eve of St Agnes,* an abuse of respectable morality. Hazlitt's work, according to an article in the *New Monthly Magazine* in November 1818, helped to 'scatter the seeds of infidelity, disaffection and licentiousness'. Like other conservative newspapers and journals, the *New Monthly Magazine* wanted to make a connection between Hazlitt's political values and sexual libertinism. The advocate of liberty was also a dangerous seducer. He threatened disorder in politics and in the proper conduct of sexual life.

Hazlitt did have his defenders, notably in the *Examiner,*

and he also knew how to attack his opponents with his own scathing words. But the attacks on his reputation as a writer and on his moral character became relentless. From 1818 onwards he was targeted on a monthly basis. He was even accused of cheating his public financially. His books were not original, it was maintained, but republished material that had already been given as lectures or published in newspapers and magazines. So, he was, in effect, asking his public to pay for the same material twice over.

Hazlitt's failed marriage was only one episode in a turbulent sexual history. In 1803, when he was still an aspiring portrait painter on a visit to Wordsworth and Coleridge in the Lake District, Hazlitt had been forced to make a hurried get-away as a result of some sexual encounters that had gone seriously wrong. What exactly happened has never been clear. But Wordsworth let Crabb Robinson, one of the great literary gossips of the early nineteenth century, in on this secret episode in Hazlitt's scandalous past, and Robinson gave Wordsworth's version of this event in a diary entry for June 15th, 1815.

The two men had been discussing Hazlitt's unflattering review of Wordsworth's long poem, *The Excursion*, which had just been published. Wordsworth chose this moment to tell Robinson why he avoided Hazlitt's company:

It appears that Hazlitt, when at Keswick, narrowly escaped being ducked by the populace, and probably sent to prison for some gross attacks on women (He even whipped one woman, *more puerorum*, for not yielding to his wishes).

This lurid account reflects the hostility that both Robinson and Wordsworth felt towards Hazlitt by 1815. As so often at this time, politics played a role in personal judgements. Neither of the two men sympathised with Hazlitt's radicalism. Both men believed that his political beliefs had cut him adrift from conventional sexual morality.

There was something about Hazlitt's sexual life that respectable men, like Crabb Robinson and Wordsworth, found, or pretended to find, offensive. Writing much earlier, in 1803, Coleridge had made a blunter assessment. In a letter to his patrons, the Wedgwoods, he had described Hazlitt as 'addicted to women, as objects of sexual indulgence'.

The Keswick episode appeared to reveal Hazlitt as a sexual predator, whose frustration could rapidly turn to violence. In a later diary entry Crabb Robinson classified him in a different but equally scandalous way: 'Like other gross sensualists, he had a horror of the society of ladies, especially of smart and handsome and modest young women...'

Others, however, saw the episode differently. Wordsworth had told the same story to one of Hazlitt's oldest and kindest friends, Charles Lamb. And in a letter written in reply in December 1814, Lamb took a much more relaxed and comic view of the episode:

The 'scapes of the great god Pan who appeared among your mountains some dozen years since, and his narrow chance of being submerged by the swains, afforded me much pleasure. I can conceive the water nymphs pulling for him.

Lamb's words are an attempt to tease Wordsworth out of his indignation and scandal mongering. In his view, what happened in Keswick was a young man's comic sexual misadventure.

As for Hazlitt, he had by 1820 developed his own analysis of his relationship with women. It was one that put writers in an uneasy relation to love at first sight. A number of his essays and reviews return to portraits of authors in love and, in each of them, there is an element of

disguised autobiography. Sometimes the writer is presented as comically inept and tongue-tied. Time spent at the
desk makes writers bad at small talk. 'Introduce him to a
tea-party of milliner's girls and they are ready to split their
sides with laughing at him,' he wrote in an 1820 essay.

Five years earlier, in an essay *On the Literary Character*, he
had presented another side of the problem. As he saw it,
authors dwelt so much in the world of imagination and
ideas that they became indifferent to 'real persons and
things'. One result was that love in a book was more satis-
fying than love in a life. Women in the flesh were never as
beautiful or as graceful as women found in words, images
and stories.

This separation of imaginary and real worlds, according
to Hazlitt, had a number of consequences. Authors experienced their emotions with a view to putting them into
memorable words. They, in fact, lived their lives twice
over, once in experience and the second in how that experience could be transformed into words. The second life —
the life transformed by language — was more important
than the first. Emotions came to them reheated and intensified by language in ways that produced a delay in the
effect of any particular feeling. 'The blow', as Hazlitt put
it, 'is felt only by reflection, the rebound is fatal.'

Another consequence was that living in an imaginary world condemned authors to a kind of 'half life'. They wandered through society like so many ancient mariners, experiencing what Hazlitt described as a 'living death; a dim twilight existence'. But it also turned them into libertines. The pleasures of the mind and imagination are tenuous and become tedious through repetition. They cannot produce the kinds of satisfaction that come from physical pleasure. Bodily pleasure may last only for a moment but Hazlitt claims 'when it returns it is as good as new'. Living a life of ideas did not lead to a detachment from physical appetites. It intensified them.

By 1820, Hazlitt did not believe that his profession suited him to either wooing women or marrying them. Authors were an awkward combination of the libertine and the dreamer, falling in love with fictions and then craving satisfaction for the desires that these fictions stimulated but did not fully satisfy. His own experience had led him back to the belief that he was fundamentally at odds with the life around him. The break-up of his marriage, his troubled sexual life, the constant attacks by his opponents, and the fragility of his literary career – all these seemed to confirm the sense that he was not destined for any happiness. And yet, with his assertion that authors and love don't mix, there is a mute appeal, as though Hazlitt was inviting someone or something to prove him wrong. He might, after all, be the exception to his own descriptions of the fate of authors in love. The intensity of his disappointment at the events of the past might turn into its opposite: a special entitlement to happiness.

In the weeks following their first meeting, Sarah Walker seemed to be the proof that he wanted but hardly dared define. He convinced himself that her gaze at their first meeting had created a special intimacy between them. She would show that there was still a possibility for a new life for him in his middle age.

CHAPTER TWO
WINTERSLOW

These early weeks of intimacy were brought to a halt in September, when Hazlitt left Southampton Buildings and Sarah. However intense his feelings for her, he was not willing to give up his professional routine – but their separation did not last long.

From 1818 onwards Hazlitt had regularly stayed at a large coaching inn, Winterslow Hut on the south-eastern edge of Salisbury Plain. Staying there gave him the time to write and had the added advantage of being on one of the main mail routes out of London. Hazlitt could keep in touch with his publishers and editors; they could send him proofs and he could prepare new copy. A letter he sent in September to Robert Baldwin, the publisher of the *London*

Magazine, gives a picture of the writer at work:

> I am now down at Winterslow Hut, where I should
> take it as a favour if you would transmit the proof of
> *Table Talk*, no 3. I should be mortified not to have it
> in the next number. I am busy transcribing Nos IV,
> V, VI, VII and VIII... If I thought they would be reg-
> ularly inserted, I would finish the whole 40 nos. out
> of hand...

This letter is typical of Hazlitt's professional correspondence. He was eager to get things into print and edgy
about any editorial decision that might prevent him from
appearing before his readers. He needed the short-term
reassurance that proofs were on the way, and was keen to
establish some long-term guarantees about publication,
not least because of the financial security it could give him.
He wanted a publisher to invest in him over time. At this
stage, he hadn't found one.

But Winterslow Hut was more than Hazlitt's version of
a writer's retreat. The village of Winterslow was within
walking distance of the inn, and it was here that Hazlitt had
lived with his wife Sarah, shortly after they were married
in 1808. Sarah's family, the Stoddarts, owned property in

the village, including the cottage that the couple had lived in until 1812. His son William had been born there in 1811. And Sarah and their son were still living in Winterslow in the summer following her separation from Hazlitt at the end of 1819.

The September trip to Winterslow almost certainly involved a visit to Sarah and William. Hazlitt had no wish to sever all connections with his wife. Four years older than her husband, Sarah Hazlitt was a well-read and independently minded woman, who was under no illusions about her husband's character and his tendency towards romantic infatuation. She also knew, however, that his son was an important figure in Hazlitt's emotional life. He was a loving if not especially responsible or conscientious father, and he enjoyed his son's company. They took walks together in the countryside around Winterslow and in London. When they were living in London, Hazlitt had taken the young William to his various haunts, and upset his wife by introducing him to the street life of the city.

As a result of their failed marriage, Hazlitt and Sarah had separately courted their son's affections and William became a domineering child, accustomed to getting his own way. In a letter of 1819, the poet John Keats described William as 'the little Nero' and Crabb Robinson described him as a 'troublesome and forward child'. But there is no evidence that Hazlitt saw his son in this way. The break-up of his marriage separated him from a child he loved, and distance made that love all the more keen and anxious.

By early October, Hazlitt was back in London and back at 9 Southampton Buildings. He had completed the work he needed to do for the *London Magazine*. One of the essays he had worked on at Winterslow, *On the Conversation of Authors,* came out in the September issue and more followed in the next few months.

His breakfast routine with Sarah resumed. She continued to come into his sitting room and Hazlitt continued to try and persuade her that they were in love. Sometimes she seemed willing to caress him. At others she maintained her distance, waiting on him while he ate, curious to hear more of the conversation that she admitted to liking. Their physical intimacy did not alter the guarded and brief responses she gave to Hazlitt's talk.

Though Sarah's reticence was at first reassuring to Hazlitt, it became increasingly tormenting. At the beginning of their affair it was for him an aspect of her erotic sweetness and innocence. Sarah did not add to that great weight of adverse judgement which he felt, with good reason, surrounded him. She offered him attention without demands. Quiet and reticent, she could easily be absorbed into the pictures created by his imagination. Her appearance each day gave Hazlitt the illusion of a domestic life. There were moments when she seemed to him like an attentive young wife. That, at least, was how he liked to remember her best: '...in her morning gown, in her dirt and her mob-cap; it is so that she has oftenest sat on my knee with her arms round my neck.' Full of erotic promise but also unthreatening, Sarah could simultaneously be Hazlitt's soul-mate and his servant. She was, at last, the woman who could share his private world without condemning him for his failures.

Hazlitt wanted his love for Sarah to develop into a lasting relationship. Given his history of brief and imaginary passions, this was a new development. It was also at odds with one of his beliefs about love and writers. In 1815, he had argued that the love of the Italian poet Petrarch for his beloved Laura was not diminished by the fact that there was no lasting intimacy between them:

The love of a man like Petrarch would have been less in character if it had been less ideal. For the purpose of inspiration a single interview was quite sufficient. The smile, which sank into his heart the first time he

ever beheld her, played around her lips ever after…
Even death could not dissolve the fine illusion: for
that which exists in the imagination is alone imperishable…

Love at first sight is enough because the feelings at first
meeting give love in its ideal form. Repeated meetings
threaten a falling away from the excitement of a first
encounter. The only guarantee of love's survival is that 'its
fine illusion' will endure in the writer's imagination and be
incarnated in his work.

At a later stage in his attempt to estabish a relationship
with her, Hazlitt would come to imagine his love for Sarah
in this way, and then doubt what his imagination told him.
But at this early stage he was still hungry for something
else, not just ideal beauty but domestic bliss. He didn't
want the permanence of imperishable ideals; he wanted
the conviction that someone else would love him for the
long term and be willing to marry him. As Hazlitt coaxed
Sarah into regarding him as her suitor, love became for him
a matter of strategy as well as passion and imagination.

The need for strategy was evident enough. Hazlitt was
trying to persuade a woman half his age into a permanent
liaison that would not compromise her respectability. His

celebrity, and the originality of his conversation may have attracted her, but he was still a married man. It was possible to get a divorce, but that would require protracted discussions with his wife and time spent in Scotland where divorce was legally recognised in a way that wasn't the case in England. Hazlitt no doubt tried to convince Sarah and himself that marriage was a possibility. He needed to act towards her as if she could be his bride. There had to be a delicate pretence between them, as though something that might happen in the future should inform their feelings for each other in the present. Otherwise their relationship was in danger of becoming stale and repetitive, a connection at best based on tea, talk and kisses in his sitting room.

One way of courting Sarah was by giving her gifts, which is likely to have started within a few months of their first meeting. They included 'a little Prayer Book, bound in crimson velvet with green silk linings', which Hazlitt remembered 'she kissed twenty times... and said... was the prettiest present in the world'. He gave her a flute, a silk shawl, tickets to the theatre and a little statue of Napoleon. In an unpublished section of *Liber Amoris*, he described another more intimate and expensive gift, '...upwards of £30 worth – a trifle among others – is my hair in a golden heart which I see set down in the Jeweller's bill...'

He also gave her copies of his books, 'three volumes of my own writings... on different occasions', likely to be *Lectures on the Dramatic Literature of the Age of Elizabeth*, a work published a few months before he moved into Southampton Buildings, and perhaps the two volumes of his essays, *Table Talk*, published in April 1821 and June 1822. The one thing we know that Sarah gave him was a locket of her hair that he wore around his neck.

Whatever his motives – to impress, educate, flatter or make up with Sarah – gift-giving became a ritual in their relationship. Her acceptance of a gift was a sign of her acceptance of him, or, at least, an acknowledgement of his role as her suitor. A gift received by her was like an assurance; something that she would take away from the room where they met, a way of establishing an association even when they were not physically together. But her pleased acceptance of his gifts did not imply any lasting commitment on her part. If we take Hazlitt's *Liber Amoris* as a guide, his gifts did not prompt her into any confession of love for him. Her actions suggested that she loved him but that his situation as a married man meant she couldn't put into words what she truly felt.

If Southampton Buildings meant one thing for Hazlitt and another for Sarah, the same was true of the world beyond the lodging house. In the early nineteenth century, Holborn was an intermediary zone between the rough and the respectable. St. Giles, one of the London 'rookeries' – a place of slums, brothels and houses for fencing stolen goods – was close by. At the same time the area was one of the centres of professional education in the city. The Inns of Court were not far from Southampton Buildings. Barristers and solicitors had their offices and chambers in and around the Inns of Court and they were supported by various trades: stationers and law booksellers, tailors and clerks. Hazlitt's rooms in Southampton Buildings were quiet, but Holborn's streets were noisy and crowded. Sarah seldom left home unaccompanied and, when she did, it was usually to visit her grandmother who lived in Somers Town, two miles to the north-west of Southampton Buildings.

For Hazlitt, London was a city of work and pleasure. Southampton Buildings was a good place for him to be, not far from the theatres of Drury Lane and Covent Garden where he went to gather material for his drama reviews. The Southampton Coffee House, round the corner from his lodgings, was one of his favourite haunts. And he played fives at a court in St. Martin's Street, a few minutes' walk away. Numerous booksellers and publishers lived nearby.

William Hone, the publisher of Hazlitt's *Political Essays*, had an office in the Old Bailey. Holywell Street, on the site of what is now Aldwych, was known as Bookseller's Row, the centre of London's second-hand book trade. Hazlitt had plenty of material near at hand.

But on the shadier side, the major theatres at Drury Lane and Covent Garden, which Hazlitt regularly visited in his capacity as a drama critic, were notorious as places where sex as well as drama was for sale. Early nineteenth-century London had a thriving sex industry. In 1830 it has been estimated that about 80,000 prostitutes were working the capital's streets.

According to Patmore, Hazlitt picked up prostitutes frequently, and was well known and well liked by them. In his memoir, first published in 1855, Patmore recalled a night walk through London that the two men made shortly after they first met in 1818.

At this early stage of their relationship, Patmore was still nervous of Hazlitt. He had been led to believe that the person he would encounter was 'an incarnate fiend'. Instead he met an emaciated and disconsolate figure who wanted to talk to him about lecturing at the Surrey Institute. The two men had once had a falling-out over an article Patmore had published, so he was surprised by

Hazlitt's willingness to talk to him as they walked together through central London. When they reached Whitehall, their conversation was interrupted by a group of prostitutes:

> Here however we met with a rather unseemly interruption, in the form of sundry petitioners; and I shall never forget the air of infantine simplicity with which Hazlitt received and answered them. That I should see anything exceptionable in the acquaintance seemed not to enter his thoughts; but his surprise and horror were extreme at the breach of etiquette committed by his unhappy protégées, in thus addressing him in the presence of a third person. And the feeling was evidently not on his own account, but on mine.

Patmore's memoir, though sympathetic to Hazlitt, is an unflinching portrait of its subject. He presents the Whitehall encounter as something he is obliged to tell, given his commitment to revealing the truth about Hazlitt's personality. Hazlitt found a psychological as well as a physical comfort with prostitutes. Patmore had his own explanation for this. Hazlitt was haunted by his enemies' dark descriptions of him – they had created a monster. And he thought that the way women, especially educated women, responded to him would be affected by the way his enemies portrayed him. Prostitutes, on the other hand, would be ignorant of this reputation. If anything, they offered him a way of escaping its oppressive power.

Patmore's anecdote suggests that Hazlitt did not simply use prostitutes for sex. Perhaps he projected onto them his own feelings about being an outcast from the respectable world. He was a friendly face to a group of women who were reviled and exploited by polite society. He gave them money, when he had any, out of sympathy and charity:

> His forbearance and charity for the 'unfortunate' persons in question were without limits; and he did not care if all the world knew it, and witnessed the results that ensued whenever his pocket was on a par with his humanity in this respect.

***

Hazlitt stayed in Southampton Buildings for a couple of months but was travelling again by mid-December 1820.

He went to his family home in Crediton, in Devon, for his first meeting with his mother Grace, and sister Penny, since his father had died in July. From Crediton he went back to Winterslow Hut where he wrote more *Table Talk* essays and visited his wife and son.

This time Hazlitt was away from Sarah for at least six weeks. His mother and sister had not been happy at the news of Hazlitt's separation from his wife. And, at the time of his father's death, Hazlitt had been hard to find. Some emotional repair work was in order. He did not want to offend his family, but at the same time he felt set on a course that was not going to meet with their approval.

Hazlitt stayed at Crediton until the January 12th, 1821. By the 18th he was certainly at Winterslow Hut because this is the date and location he gave for the composition of one of his most celebrated essays, *On Living to One Self*. The essay begins with a genial evocation of Hazlitt's mood and circumstance as he sits by the fireside at Winterslow Hut and prepares to write:

I never was in a better place or humour than I am at present for writing on this subject. I have a partridge getting ready for my supper, my fire is blazing on the hearth, the air is mild for the season of the year, I

have had but a slight fit of indigestion today… I have
three good hours before me and therefore I will
attempt it…

This intimate, ironic self-portrait of the writer at work
suggests a figure at home in his world. The essay itself is an
attempt to sustain this serenity of tone in the face of everything that might threaten it. Hazlitt meditates on the costs
of worldly ambition and success. His ideal of 'living to one
self' – being in the world but not of it – is a form of self-
immunisation. Hazlitt argues that an anonymous life, one
removed from the brittle satisfactions of living in 'the
reflection of his own image in the public gaze', is best.
Personal and public life are equally insecure. Any happiness
that depends upon friendship, marriage or love is precarious. It is at this moment in Hazlitt's meditation that Sarah
appears, indirectly but unmistakably:

He who looks at beauty to admire, to adore it, who
reads of its wondrous powers in novels, in poems or
in plays is not unwise; but let no man fall in love for
from that moment he is 'the baby of a girl'.

To be the 'baby of a girl' is to lose that immunity to the

world and its disappointments that is produced by 'living to one self'. And Hazlitt returns to a quotation from his friend, the writer Barry Procter, a quotation that became strongly associated in his mind with the figure of Sarah:

> With what a wavering air she goes
> Along the corridor! How like a faun!

In *On Living to One Self,* Hazlitt warns against the enticements of a 'wavering air'. It may be safe to fantasise about an imaginary woman in this way, but not to entangle the fantasy with any woman who might be taken for the real life equivalent of the fantasy: '... defend me from meeting the original' is how he puts it in the essay, in a tone that implies he already knows the danger of confusing fantasy and reality.

Sarah is associated in *On Living to One Self* with all the things that threaten Hazlitt's ideal of living a life that acknowledges others but does not depend upon them for approval or affection. It suggests that, within six months of their first meeting, he was having some serious second thoughts.

A letter that Sarah wrote to Hazlitt in January 1821 shows another aspect of the distance between them:

Sir,

Doctor Read sent the *London Magazine*, with compli-
ments and thanks, no Letters or Parcels except the
one which I have sent with the Magazines according
to your directions. Mr. Lamb sent for the things
which you left in our care likewise a cravat which
was not with them – I send my thanks for your kind
offer but must decline accepting it – Baby is quite
well, the first floor is occupied at present, it is very
uncertain when it will be disengaged.

My Family send their best respects to You. I hope
your little son is quite well
From Yours Respectfully
S. Walker

Sarah was not at this point in any mood for an amorous
exchange of letters. She sounds like an efficient secretary
responding to various demands from her boss. She might
have been close to Hazlitt in his sitting room in
Southampton Buildings, but whatever happened there
happened in a place apart, cut off from other aspects of
her life. Nothing in this letter suggests that Hazlitt had
remotely succeeded in making her see their relationship in
any other way.

Like later letters Sarah sent to him, its business-like tone depressed Hazlitt. It seemed to strengthen a recurrent disenchantment with love that surfaces in *On Living to Oneself*. But there was another side, and one that shows Hazlitt's capacity to imagine himself in rapidly changing moods. If he was sceptical about love at this point, he also liked to ignore his doubts. Early in 1821 he reworked *The Past and the Future*, an essay he had withdrawn from publication because it was too much like a piece already published by Charles Lamb, and added passages to it where Sarah again makes a thinly disguised appearance. Hazlitt becomes the melancholy lover, wholly dependent for his well-being on imagining his beloved:

> Without that face pale as the primrose with hyacinthine locks, forever shining and forever haunting me, mocking my waking thoughts as in a dream, without that smile which my heart could never turn to scorn, without those eyes dark with their own lustre, still bent on mine, and drawing the soul into their liquid mazes like a sea of love... What should I do, how pass away the listless leaden hours?

The self imagined here is like Keats's knight in *La Belle*

Dame sans Merci, a poem Hazlitt had almost certainly read. Both are absorbed by a vision of love, resigned to dreaming their lives away in delicious, unobtainable fantasies. The ideal of self-sufficiency presented in *On Living to Oneself* has given way to its opposite. Being the 'baby of a girl' has its own gloomy attractions.

On Living to Oneself and *Past and Future* are amongst the first of the many occasions that Sarah was to make an appearance in Hazlitt's work. His fascination with her had a double life made up of his meetings with her in person and his recreations of their love life in his writing. Writing about her grew out of their physical separation and increasingly seemed to require it. This alone doesn't explain why Hazlitt spent so much time away from Sarah while he was in love with her. That had as much to do with his tenderness for his son and the requirements of his professional routine. But it does suggest that falling in love for Hazlitt was a literary as well as an emotional event. Writing about love and being in love entered into an intoxicating and potentially damaging exchange that was to have serious and bizarre consequences not just for him, but also for Sarah and their respective families.

CHAPTER THREE
ON HOLD

By mid-February 1821, Hazlitt was back again in London and back again in his rooms at 9 Southampton Buildings. Sarah resumed her role as Hazlitt's servant and intimate companion. Breakfast and kisses came together again. But the doubts that had so clearly surfaced at the end of 1820 had not been overcome. Sarah remained guarded and Hazlitt remained passionately ambivalent.

At some point in the late winter or early spring of 1821, Sarah told him about her continuing love for a man she was no longer able to see. 'Pride of birth' had prevented him from continuing the affair. The story Sarah told was a reversal of her older sister's experience and, whatever its truth, it allowed a temporary and fragile compromise between her and Hazlitt. He was moved by the idea of Sarah's continuing fidelity to a man who was unable to return her love because of the difference in social class between them. She became to him like a literary heroine, whose love was just for one man. If the love he had hoped for was no longer a possibility, perhaps something very close to it was, a special kind of friendship based on affection and mutual esteem. She might even acknowledge that what he felt for her was similar to what she felt for her departed lover. They would find fulfilment in their shared disappointment. In the event, Sarah was willing to agree to this compromise, which helped Hazlitt balance his love for her with his ideal of 'living to one self': it seemed as if the basis for something that would last had been reached between them.

Events, and Hazlitt's preoccupations as an author, made this compromise seem like a good idea, at least for the early months of 1821. On March 6th, Sarah's youngest brother, John Anthony, died. He was three years old. Other children had died young in the Walker family. Their experience was not exceptional in a period when one in every ten children died in infancy. But no child's death is simply a matter of routine. Sarah and her family mourned their loss, and, although Hazlitt made no direct comment on this in his letters, Sarah's reference in her January letter to 'Baby' being 'quite well' may have come in response to his concern about John Anthony's health.

A month earlier there had been a very different kind of death. John Scott, Hazlitt's long-standing colleague and the editor of the *London Magazine*, was mortally wounded in a duel provoked by some heated words between Scott and Hazlitt's old antagonist, *Blackwood's Magazine*. Scott had demanded to know what the connection was between *Blackwood's Magazine* and John Lockhart, a lawyer and writer. It was in fact known that Lockhart was a writer and, informally, an editor for the magazine but the conventions of the time required that these connections remained anonymous. Lockhart, like other contributors to *Blackwood's*, was always up for a fight, especially if it generated the kind of scandal that would increase sales, and he demanded an apology from Scott for his impertinence in identifying him by name. If that was not forthcoming he demanded a duel.

Hazlitt was aware of this burgeoning row. He had written to Scott from Crediton in January when he was staying with his mother and sister. Typically, the letter is mostly about proof corrections and the work that Hazlitt wanted to do for the *London Magazine*. But he added a short passage urging Scott not to give in. Hazlitt had, after all, stood up to *Blackwood's* two years previously when he had sued them as a result of their attempt to destroy his reputation.

A few days after Hazlitt wrote his letter, Scott received a visit from Lockhart's proxy in London, a young lawyer called Christie. Christie accused Scott of cowardice because he would not go to Edinburgh and confront Lockhart. Scott was insulted by Christie and challenged him to a duel. On February 16th, the two men met in a field in Chalk Farm near Hampstead. Scott fired his pistol and missed. Christie wounded Scott in the shoulder. Eleven days later he was dead.

Nobody involved in the quarrel had remotely imagined that things would turn out this way. Patmore, Scott's second in the duel, was blamed for letting things get out of control. As for Hazlitt, he had lost a valued colleague. Scott had published some of Hazlitt's early art criticism and political essays. Then a rift had occurred between the two men, the result of an editorial Scott had written attacking Hazlitt's character. The two did not meet again until January 1820 when Hazlitt had started to contribute to the newly founded *London Magazine*. Whatever Scott's reservations about Hazlitt's morals, he respected his talent as a writer and was pleased with the drama reviews and essays he submitted. Scott's death raised a question mark over the magazine's future. Hazlitt was in danger of losing an outlet for his work, one that welcomed the personal and digressive style of his essays, and an important source of income.

In early March, news of another death reached London, this time of the poet John Keats who had died in Rome on the February 23rd. Hazlitt and Keats were never close friends, but Keats's admiration for Hazlitt was unstinting. In a letter to his brothers, written in January 1818, Keats had described Hazlitt's 'depth of Taste' as one of 'the three things superior in the modern world'. Both men had been vilified in *Blackwood's* as members of the Cockney School of Writers. As far as Hazlitt was concerned, Keats had been crucified by 'The Cockney School' label. A capricious public had been turned against the poet by the vilification of his work. Hazlitt saw parallels with his own situation. So far he had been resilient enough to survive the onslaught, but he was convinced that, like Keats, the sales of his work had been badly affected by hostile reviews.

If the death of Sarah's young brother was a cause for sadness, the deaths of Scott and Keats were also inauspicious signs for Hazlitt's professional life. They seemed to mark the triumph of a mean-minded and vengeful culture that wanted to crush the values that Hazlitt most wanted to defend. Further depressing news came in late May. Napoleon had died in exile on the island of St. Helena. Hazlitt's response this time was not as extreme as it had been when he heard the news of Napoleon's defeat at Waterloo. Then, according to the painter Robert Haydon, Hazlitt had seemed prostrated in mind and body, walking about 'unwashed, unshaved, hardly sober by day, and always intoxicated by night, literally, without exaggeration, for weeks'. In 1821 Hazlitt did not make a public display of his grief. Napoleon's death got one brief but telling mention in an essay about metropolitan conversation, *On Coffee House Politicians*, first published in 1822. In it he recalled an obscure journalist called Mudford:

> But I thought of him the other day when the news of the death of Buonaparte came, whom we both loved for precisely contrary reasons, he for putting down the rabble of the people, and I because he put down the rabble of kings.

Napoleon was, in Hazlitt's idea of him, the last great defender of the revolutionary values of liberty, equality and fraternity. And these were linked to another value that Napoleon represented: he had come from an obscure background to become the ruler of a great nation. None of his power or standing came from inherited wealth or status. This answered to Hazlitt's sense of his own obscure origins and to the fierceness of his ambition. One of his characteristic gestures, his hand slipped into his waistcoat, echoed Napoleon's. The little statue of Napoleon on the mantelpiece in his sitting room in Southampton Buildings was a visible sign of his continuing admiration, and it was one of the few possessions he kept with him.

Shortly after Scott's death, Hazlitt took over as a temporary editor of the *London Magazine*, working with its owner Robert Baldwin, until it was sold later that year to its new owners, the publishers Taylor and Hessey. He was preoccupied by the publication in April of the first volume of *Table Talk or Original Essays*. Hazlitt had already been publishing essays under the title *Table Talks* in the *London Magazine*. But only two previously published pieces appeared in the book. The other eleven essays appeared for the first time. By using the title *Table Talk*, Hazlitt wanted to bring his magazine readership to the book. Sensitive to the criticism that he recycled material, he wanted to reassure them that what they were getting was 'original'.

But something else was at work in the claim to originality. Hazlitt was announcing to the world a new identity as an author. He no longer wanted to be perceived as a writer of criticism, reviews and political polemics. Instead, he was experimenting with a new form. His 'original' essays combined epigrams, quotations and anecdotes that could be about anything and everything. Their conversational style gave him the freedom to improvise and digress and to write autobiographically. Hazlitt was one of the first close readers of English Romantic poetry. He wanted to bring to his prose essays the intimacy and emotional directness that he found in the best work of the Romantics.

The new book met with mixed reviews. The *London Magazine* promptly praised it and its author, describing Hazlitt as a 'man of undoubted and original mind'. His method of 'consulting his own nature' in the essays was a route to a new kind of truthfulness about the self. Thomas Noon Talfourd, one of Hazlitt's younger admirers, followed this praise with a lengthy review in the May issue, in which he was particularly struck by how Hazlitt's essays moved beyond the conventional boundaries of criticism: 'They do not merely guide us in our estimates of the work of others... but they give us pieces of sentiment themselves worthy of a high place in the chambers of memory.'

Equally predictably, Hazlitt's old antagonists soon took notice of the book and, once started, the denunciations took a long time to stop. If there was anything original about the book it was simply that it displayed all of Hazlitt's failings more clearly than before. A grudging acceptance of the quality of some of the essays did not stop extended complaints, as in the July issue of the *New Edinburgh Review*, about the 'vilest indelicacy and slang' in Hazlitt's style. The June issue of the *British Critic* noticed the melancholic mood in many of the essays and suggested that Hazlitt would be best helped by picking 'him out of his envelope, just as we would rout a grub from a snug lodging in his cocoon'. In August, *Blackwood's* published a parody of a *Table Talk* essay and in October the *Quarterly Review* described them as 'crude though belaboured lucubrations'. Some of his opinions showed 'insane extravagance'. Hazlitt was a 'Slang-whanger', 'one who makes use of political or other garble, vulgarly called slang, that serves to amuse the rabble'. Hazlitt's conversational style, as far as these reviewers were concerned, was the demonstration of a terrible lapse in taste.

The publication of *Table Talk* produced another, more personal controversy, one that demonstrated Hazlitt's disregard for the distinction between what might be argued about amongst friends and what might end up in a book. His sense of the world's injustice provoked him to fierce and searching political criticisms of tyranny and unearned privilege. But his identification with the suffering of others could rapidly turn into an aggrieved sense of the injustices inflicted on him. Feeling wronged by others, Hazlitt felt justified in offending them in return, and not just in conversations and letters, but in public print. In two essays in *Table Talk* — *On Paradox and Commonplace* and *On People with One Idea* — Hazlitt attacked two of his political allies, Shelley and Leigh Hunt. He described Shelley as a 'philosophical fanatic' who was convinced that 'whatever is, is wrong'. The poet had a 'fire in his eye, a fever in his blood, a maggot in his brain, a hectic flutter in his speech'. Leigh Hunt was described by Hazlitt as an egotist: voluble, eloquent, but basically always talking about himself.

Hazlitt had met Shelley briefly in 1817, but the two men were not friends. It was not just that Hazlitt distrusted the intensity of Shelley's idealism. He also thought that Shelley's privileged social background protected him from the kinds of public attack that he and Keats had suffered. With Leigh Hunt it was a different matter. The two had first met in 1814, when Hunt was in prison for publishing a libel against the Prince of Wales. Hazlitt became a

regular visitor at Hunt's different homes in London. The
Examiner, the paper edited by Hunt and his brother John,
published Hazlitt's work and defended his reputation.

Hunt was hurt by Hazlitt's attack and let him know it.
In April, Hazlitt wrote to Hunt to make an apology of
sorts. But the letter is as much about Hazlitt's sense of
grievance as it is about any offence caused to his friend. In
it he claimed that he had not got a proper return for the
kindness he had shown to other writers. He itemised the
ways in which he had praised Hunt and complained that
Hunt had failed to reciprocate. Hazlitt had expected Hunt
to attend his lectures and wasn't convinced by Hunt's
explanation of why he hadn't – his claim that he couldn't
be seen to promote writers who had promoted him struck
Hazlitt as another example of an excuse masquerading as a
principle.

The April letter is a testament to the nervous rivalries
that informed Hazlitt's friendship with other writers. He
often felt personally betrayed by people who were suppos-
edly his political allies. But the strangest thing in this letter
is Hazlitt's indifference to one of the things that had most
upset Hunt – that his friend had criticised him *in public*:

You provoke me into thinking hard things of you and

then you wonder that I hitch them into an Essay, as
if that made any difference...

It was this very 'hitching things into an essay' that *did*
make a difference to Hunt, and not only because he felt
personally hurt. Their political enemies would take comfort from the spectacle, as Hunt put it in a letter to Hazlitt,
of 'brother-reformers cutting and carbonading one another in public'.

Hunt responded generously to Hazlitt's letter and the
'brother-reformers' settled their difference. If wounded,
Hazlitt felt satisfied if he could wound in return and writing an essay was one way of doing this. On his side Hunt
did not want to continue the quarrel. He felt an 'irrepressible love for [Hazlitt] on account of his sympathy for
mankind, his unmercenary disinterestedness, and his suffering'. But Hunt went on to make a significant qualifica-
tion. There was something detached in his affection for
Hazlitt. It was based on shared political beliefs and a sympathetic recognition of the fact that Hazlitt seemed
doomed to be unhappy. A more personal affection was
impossible because Hazlitt would not allow it. He was,
according to Hunt, settled in his chronic suspicion of other
people's motives and emotions, declaring by his behaviour

that 'I have no faith in anything, especially your advances...
we have nothing in common between us'.

Hunt's willingness to patch things up with Hazlitt left a
bitter after-taste. Hunt found it hard to reconcile himself
to what he regarded as Hazlitt's habit of giving publicity to
opinions that should be best left private: 'If I have teased
you, as you say, I have never revenged myself by trampling
upon you in public...'

There is no record of what Sarah Walker thought of the
book. It is very likely that Hazlitt gave her a copy of *Table
Talk*. If she read it, she would have discovered that she was
becoming, in however veiled a way, a character in Hazlitt's
writing. Adoring passages about the 'face pale as the prim-
rose with hyacinthine locks' alternated with warnings
about becoming 'the baby of a girl': if she read them she
may have been flattered but her reactions to Hazlitt in the
months following the publication suggest that she wasn't.

Hazlitt stayed in London during April and May of 1821.
He wrote essays for the *London Magazine* and encouraged
his friends, including Hunt, to do the same. But he was
unwilling to take on full editorial responsibility for the
magazine and in late April its owner, Robert Baldwin,
agreed to sell it to John Taylor and Robert Hessey, the
publishers of Keats and John Clare amongst others. Hazlitt

continued to write for the *London,* but he did not feel as closely involved in its direction as he had under John Scott's editorship.

By early June, Hazlitt was back in Winterslow Hut and away from Sarah again. His letters from this period show signs of mental strain. He failed to meet a deadline for an article for the *London Magazine*. In a letter of explanation to Taylor and Hessey he complained of being 'but indifferent since I came here'. His mood was not helped by Taylor's rejection of an essay Hazlitt had written on Guy Fawkes. In it he had defended Guy Fawkes as a figure willing to risk his life for his religion. The tone of the essay was abrasive, as though Hazlitt delighted in taking a view that he knew would provoke his readers. He agreed with Taylor to 'alter it or try another experiment on some less obnoxious subject', but instead found another outlet for the essay. It was published across three issues of the *Examiner* in November.

The rejection of his essay was not the only reason for Hazlitt's low spirits. The special friendship that he had agreed with Sarah earlier in the year, and the reverence he wanted to feel for her devotion to a previous love, were in practice proving hard to sustain. They amounted to little more than excuses for Sarah to keep him at arm's length. It left Hazlitt in the position of a sympathetic brother or father rather than a lover. Loving Sarah because she loved someone else was getting him nowhere.

If Hazlitt was becoming vexed about the question of his future with Sarah, his visits to Winterslow were also concerned with settling the future of someone else whose love he wanted: his son William. Since the separation from his wife, Hazlitt had lost the continuous contact with his son that had once played such an important part in his emotional life. His movements back and forth between London and Winterslow during this period make clear the conflict between his love for his son and his love for Sarah. In Southampton Buildings he was away from William; in Winterslow Hut he was away from her.

The question of his son's education offered a way out of this dilemma. William's tenth birthday was on September 21st, 1821. His parents needed to decide where and how he was going to continue his education. Either during his June visit to Winterslow, or when he returned in November, Hazlitt and his wife agreed that their son should be enrolled in a school in London, Dawson's Academy. Hazlitt's nephew was already a pupil there, which would provide William with a familiar contact in a new place. The arrangement increased the pressure on Hazlitt's finances. His wife was not prepared to pay the full cost of her son's education out of her annuity of £150 a year. But it would mean that for six months of each year William would be near his father in London. Dawson's Academy was in Brunswick Square, near St. Pancras, within easy walking distance of Southampton Buildings.

From late June until early December Hazlitt continued to shuttle back and forth between London and Winterslow. In early October one of the new owners of the *London Magazine*, James Hessey, visited him at Southampton Buildings to discuss future work and found Hazlitt in a combative mood. The rejection of his essay still rankled. He was not at all keen on the proposal that Hessey made to him for a series of essays on 'Living Authors'.

According to Hessey's account of the meeting, Hazlitt felt 'no interest in them or their works'. It 'cost him no effort and brought him no fame'. Instead he wanted to continue with the *Table Talk* series of his essays. Hazlitt had become suspicious of Taylor and Hessey's editorial control. He felt, according to Hessey, 'so annoyed and cramped in his mind by the fear of alteration or objection or perhaps rejection altogether that he could not write freely as he was accustomed to do'. Hazlitt's disenchantment with routine journalism was becoming more entrenched. He wanted the freedom to write in his own way and not work at the bidding of others.

CHAPTER FOUR
THE RIVAL

Another meeting in Southampton Buildings troubled Hazlitt. In the same month that he disagreed with James Hessey about his future contributions to the *London Magazine*, a new lodger rented rooms from Mrs. Walker. His name was John Tomkins; he was training to be a lawyer; and, unlike Hazlitt, he was only a couple of years older than Sarah.

Tall, handsome and gentlemanly, Tomkins rapidly became Hazlitt's rival in love. In a letter to Patmore, written in June 1822, he bitterly remembered Tomkins' arrival: 'The instant Tomkins came, she flung herself at his head in the most barefaced way, and used to run blushing and breathless to meet him.' After euphoria and uneasy compromise in his exchanges with Sarah, Hazlitt now found himself tormented by jealousy. The character of the conversation between Sarah and Hazlitt changed. He started cross-questioning her about her actions and emotions. He played over in his mind what she said and did, finding in this brooding analysis either reassurance or further agony. Jealousy laid its impossible demand on him: to prove conclusively that his own worst fantasies about Sarah were not true.

Sarah, for her part, denied that she was attracted to Tomkins. According to Hazlitt's recollection, she said that she 'despised looks' – thereby confirming in Hazlitt's mind that she had recognised Tomkins as a handsome man. She also claimed to hate Tomkins's red slippers. What was offered as a reassurance also suggested that she was curious enough about Tomkins to notice them in the first place. This was one of Hazlitt's problems in Southampton Buildings. Little details could mean a lot. A glance could hold the promise of future bliss. Mention of a pair of slippers could suggest that Sarah was attracted to someone else. Her denials of any attraction came in a way that undermined their credibility. Whatever she said fed Hazlitt's jealousy. It wasn't just Tomkins' presence and her blushes that disturbed him. He began to discover, or invent, another Sarah. The mixture of erotic sweetness and virginal purity that had charmed him in the opening months of their relationship was now replaced by a very different kind of perception.

This new image of Sarah was stimulated by a kitchen conversation Hazlitt overheard. In a letter written to Patmore in June 1822, Hazlitt gave a version, with his own commentary, of what was said between Sarah, her younger sister and brother, Betsey and Cajah, and Mrs. Walker.

Betsey was gossiping about one of Hazlitt's fellow lodgers, Mr. Griffiths, the apothecary from Wales:

Betsey: Oh! If those trousers were to come down, what a sight there would be. (A general loud laugh)
Mother: Yes! He's a proper one. Mr. Follet is nothing to him.
Mr. Cajah (aged 17): Then I suppose he must be seven inches.
Mother W: He's quite a monster! He nearly tumbled over Mr. Hazlitt one night.
Sarah (At that once, that still and ever dear name, oh! Why do I grow pale, why do I weep and forgive?) said something inaudible, but in connection.
Cajah: (Laughing) Sarah says...

Sarah: I say, Mr. Follett wears straps...

Hazlitt cut off his record of the conversation at this point; for him enough or too much had already been reported. They were talking about Mr. Griffiths' penis. Mrs. Walker and her children enjoyed gossiping about their lodgers and talking about the things they'd seen which they shouldn't have seen. There was a knowingness about this that disturbed Hazlitt deeply. Breakfast trays, morning gowns, and tender caresses were a charade. The Walkers were a family united not by their piety and respectability, but by their knowledge of sex and bodies. Or they were not one family but two: the respectable group directed by the father, and the bawdy licentious clan directed by the mother. Sarah might have known more about sex than Hazlitt cared to imagine.

Once Hazlitt was set in this frantic, jealous mood, Southampton Buildings turned into a rumour mill for him. He heard that Mrs. Walker had once hoisted up Sarah's petticoats when a footman visited the house. Worse still, this was a game that mother and daughter regularly played. Hazlitt presented to himself and others — not least to Sarah — a vision of love that was refined and delicate, a love that controlled desire as well as sought its fulfilment. What he seemed to be getting in response was something very different: love, if it existed at all, was just a name for having sexual fun and as much of it as possible. Any occasion could turn into a romp or bawdy joke.

When Hazlitt was pursuing this train of thought, Sarah became a whore, and her mother was her 'keeper', her bawd. If this was true, other disturbing possibilities presented themselves. Each revelation about the Walkers and their behaviour indicated something about Hazlitt's masculinity, or lack of it. Hazlitt had gone through an intricate courtship while all Sarah had been waiting for was the right commanding move from him. His attempts at courteous behaviour now seemed only a means for Hazlitt to hide from himself his own inadequacies as a lover.

The end of 1821 was a time of quarrels and fragile reconciliations. Hazlitt questioned Sarah, not just about Tomkins, but about other things he had heard or overheard. Sarah denied the story about the footman and the lifted petticoats, just as she had denied any attraction to Tomkins. 'You sit and fancy things out of your own head', she asserted, 'and then lay them to my charge. There is not a word of truth in your suspicions.'

At this stage, it still seemed to Hazlitt that there was a way through this turbulence. The best way of resolving his problems was not to test Sarah but to marry her. Sarah's denials of his jealous suspicions provided scant consolation. Marriage, he imagined, would give him the security he needed. But marriage with Sarah meant divorcing his wife, and he couldn't do that without her consent. The subject may have been discussed between them on Hazlitt's previous visits to Winterslow; and perhaps he brought it up again when he went down there in late November and early December of 1821.

Despite the strains in his relationship with Sarah, Hazlitt still maintained his professional routine. But, as ever, developing his career met with set backs and obstacles. On December 1st, 1821, Hazlitt wrote a letter from Winterslow Hut to his young friend Thomas Talfourd, who had taken over from Hazlitt as drama critic of the *London Magazine*. Hazlitt was increasingly worried about money. John Warren, the publisher of the first volume of *Table Talk*, had gone bankrupt, and Hazlitt wanted Talfourd to help him get an advance of £100 from Henry Colbourn, who had agreed to publish the second volume. But Hazlitt's wheeling and dealing and drumming up of advances were suddenly cut across by words of a very different kind:

The truth is, I seem to have been hurt in my mind

lately, and continued effort is too much for any patience, and mine is nearly exhausted.

These words echo the depressed conclusion to the last in a series of lectures on Elizabethan drama that Hazlitt gave in December 1819: 'Life is a continued struggle to be what we are not, and to do what we cannot.' His exhaustion was not just to do with the stresses of authorship. His rows with Sarah seemed to provide further evidence of his efforts to be something that he could not be. This is made clear in a wistful sentence that immediately followed in the same letter:

My dear Talfourd, if you have a girl that loves you and that you have regard for, lose no time in marrying and think yourself happy, whatever else may happen.

This reads like the wisdom of the bereft.

Hazlitt left Winterslow and came back to London in early December 1821. But the rapidity of his movements in the next few weeks suggest that he could scarcely bear to be in Southampton Buildings. On December 10th, he set out with Joseph Parkes, a young lawyer, to see Tom

Hickman fight with Bill Neate at Hungerford.

In the early nineteenth century, prize fights were great festive occasions that drew together people of many different social classes. Like football today, the sport was awash with bar-room experts and legendary memories. Hazlitt enjoyed sport, but he had not been to a prize fight before. It is likely that Patmore, knowing about his difficulties with Sarah, encouraged him to go. The two met up in Hungerford on the day of the fight and returned to London together on December 12th.

Hazlitt rapidly transformed this experience into one of his most famous essays, *The Fight,* first published in the *New Monthly Magazine* in February 1822. In the published version of the essay, there is only a hint of the author's personal unhappiness. Determined to leave London, and convinced that he has missed the main stagecoaches leaving for the West Country, Hazlitt decides to get a local coach as far as Brentford: 'I argued (not unwisely) that even a Brentford coachman was better company than my own thoughts (such as they were just then) and at his invitation mounted the box with him.'

This indication of personal unhappiness provides a clue to the wider mood of the essay. Although this is not explicitly stated in the published version of the essay, *The*

Fight is about the pleasures of getting away from the claus-
trophobic world of Southampton Buildings into open air
and public space. Hazlitt delighted in his journey on the
Bath Mail – once he gets on it – travelling from London to
Hungerford, 'wrapped in a great coat' and holding an
umbrella to 'keep off a drizzling mist'. He was surrounded
by the buzz and excitement of an urban crowd moving into
the countryside. He encounters outspoken characters and
then the great decisive action of the fight itself, which takes
him away from the uncertain outcomes of his love life and
the endless difficulties of finding the right words to say to
Sarah. He could, for a time, forget the 'hurt in my mind'.

In the published version of *The Fight* Hazlitt sketched a
change in his mood. He begins with a sense of his own sad
absurdity, 'putting the will for the deed and aiming at ends
without employing means', but by the end of the essay he
returns home to London 'in high spirits'.

The unpublished draft gives a much fuller account of
the essayist's mood. As he leaves London, Hazlitt lets
the reader into the 'secret' of his unhappiness in love.
Something has gone badly wrong, forcing him away from
the woman he loves into an extravagantly imagined loneliness. Sarah is identified not by her own name but as his
'Clarissa' or 'Infelice'. Literary comparisons again shape

Hazlitt's experience of love. Richardson's heroine, Clarissa, like Sarah, refused her lover's advances. Infelice was another virtuous heroine from an obscure Jacobean comedy, *The Honest Whore*, by Thomas Dekker. Like Clarissa, she resisted her father's tyrannical will but, unlike her, she did so in the name of a man she loved. These names for Sarah suggest that Hazlitt thought of her as more sinned against than sinning while he was writing his essay. If there was trouble he was the main source of it.

In the unpublished draft Hazlitt's 'high spirits' on his return to London are explicitly connected to a renewed optimism about his future with Sarah:

> Besides I had better Spirits now than before: for as the Pilgrim feels joy as he turns towards Mecca, so I felt a secret satisfaction that every mile we passed brought me nearer to Brentford and to her who is the Goddess of my idolatory...

Patmore's recollection of Hazlitt confirms this picture of someone relieved from melancholy. He wrote of the rarity of seeing Hazlitt 'for eight and forty hours together as happy as a boy or bird; as free from all seeming consciousness of the ills to which his "flesh" above all is heir to, as if some kind genius had charmed his memory and imagination to sleep.' By getting away, however briefly, from Sarah and from himself, Hazlitt was able to gain new confidence in the possibility of their life together.

But the differences between the published and the unpublished versions of *The Fight* show him grappling with another problem. If he wanted more of his autobiography in his essays he had to make decisions about how much of his life to display and how to find the right words to display it. By the end of 1821 a number of factors were likely to influence his decisions. One was Sarah's own reactions to any references to their love life in his work. Another may have been a response to the hostile remarks about the melancholy mood that some reviewers detected in the *Table Talk* essays. He did not want to be seen as 'a grub... lodging in his cocoon'. And these two things raised larger questions. If Hazlitt was going to write about himself in his essays, what kind of self did he want to present to his readers: the figure working towards composure and control that he presented in *On Living to Oneself* or someone more passionate, volatile and contradictory?

The 'high spirits' he felt on his return to London renewed Hazlitt's determination to sort out what he saw as the major barrier to his happiness with Sarah. He spent a few days in London and then went down to Winterslow for further discussions with his wife. By the end of December she had agreed to a divorce.

This would not be an easy matter. Legal divorce was not available in England in the 1820s except under exclusive and exceptional circumstances. The very wealthy could legally separate by sponsoring a private bill through Parliament, but such an action was way beyond Hazlitt's means. In Scotland things were different. There the law allowed divorce. It was an extremely rare event in early nineteenth-century Britain, but, from the late eighteenth century onwards, a small but increasing number of petitioners, mostly women, had sought divorces in Scotland.

The process was complicated. Hazlitt had to meet a residence requirement. He needed to be in Scotland for 40 days if his case was to be heard under Scottish law. The divorce would also require a special piece of theatre. Hazlitt would have to set up an adulterous liaison in Edinburgh and make sure it was witnessed. His wife would have to come to Scotland to take out a complaint against him. She would also have to take the 'Oath of Calumny', a sworn statement made before a judge that there had been no collusion between husband and wife. Without this the divorce could not be finalised. Legal wrangles could and did break out about the jurisdiction of a Scottish court over a marriage contracted in England. Scottish judges were sensitive to the fact that Edinburgh might be inundated with English couples seeking Scottish divorces. By 1820, enough cases had been heard to guide judges in their decisions and in the end most divorce petitions were granted. But the outcome was not certain. Some women suing for divorce from their husbands could be questioned closely for evidence of collusion. Sarah Hazlitt had to prepare for the possibility of an interrogation about her marriage and the circumstances of its breakdown.

In Hazlitt's mind at least, all this could be endured because it had a purpose: the creation of a new Mrs. Hazlitt. He did not have to be the hapless creature he described in *The Fight*, 'putting the will for the deed, and aiming at ends without employing means'. He began to do the opposite, planning a future and putting in place the means to realise it.

An evening at the Covent Garden theatre with Sarah and her mother reinforced Hazlitt's hopes for future happiness. On January 24th, 1822, they went to see *Romeo and Juliet*. Perhaps the play's love scenes affected their mood, but Hazlitt detected a renewed sweetness and responsiveness in Sarah's attitude towards him. He recalled this in a letter written to her the following month:

> Oh! My sitting down beside you, you whom I loved
> so well, so long, and you assuring me I had not less-
> ened your pleasure at the play by being with you,
> and giving that dear hand to press in mine – I
> seemed to be in Heaven... I sat beside the adorable
> creature by her own permission – And as I folded
> you, yes, you my best Sarah to my heart, there was,
> as you say, 'a tie between us', you did seem to be
> mine for a few short moments, in all truth & honour
> and sacredness – Oh! Could we but be always so –
> do not mock me, for I am indeed a very child in
> love.

Hazlitt hovered around Sarah at the theatre, wooing her by displays of submission. As they sat together watching the play and holding hands, he imagined Sarah as emotionally if not legally married to him. As before, his letter gives the impression of someone discovering very large meanings in very slight gestures. This timorous ecstasy was short-lived.

A few days after the visit to the theatre Hazlitt's craving for reassurance got on Sarah's nerves and they had another row in his sitting room. It may have been on this occasion that Hazlitt upbraided Sarah for the bawdy conversation and the stories about lifted petticoats and visiting footmen. Sarah lost patience with Hazlitt. He seemed, by turns, to be accusing her of being a whore and declaring that he would love her for ever. She refused his demand for a kiss and left the room.

Absurdity, it seems, had rapidly returned to his life. Hazlitt was due to leave for Scotland on January 27th to pursue a divorce so he could marry a woman who had just walked out on him. He needed some kind of assurance from Sarah that there was a bond between them. This was achieved by the little statue of Napoleon that Hazlitt kept on the mantelpiece over the fire in his sitting room. He persuaded Sarah to talk to him again and she agreed. He apologised for what he had said in the 'agony of the moment'. She reverted to an old theme of their conversations: her continuing devotion to the man who could not marry her because she was, in her own description, 'a tradesman's daughter'.

He talked to her about this abiding love: was there some similarity between him and her former lover? She ruled out that idea, but indicated that there was a likeness with the statue of Napoleon – he had been taller than

Napoleon but there was a similarity. Hazlitt immediately tried to give her the statue. She initially refused it, but then agreed to accept it, not as a gift but as something she would look after in Hazlitt's absence. The transaction released a tension between them, and they embraced. Hazlitt left Sarah with an image of a man he admired that reminded Sarah of a man she still loved. Sarah was the 'Goddess' of Hazlitt's idolatory. Now, at least, she too had an idol of sorts. If they weren't worshipping the same thing, at least they were both worshipping, and, in Sarah's case, the 'little image' that reminded her of the man she loved might also remind her, however indirectly, of Hazlitt. With this fragile memento of their relationship in place, he took the coach to Edinburgh.

CHAPTER FIVE
EDINBURGH

Hazlitt arrived in Edinburgh on February 4th. He had broken his journey from London at Stamford to visit Burleigh House, not far from the town, to write an article about the pictures housed there. During his stay Hazlitt found himself with time on his hands. As he waited for the next coach to Edinburgh he began to write down some of his conversations with Sarah. Six weeks later he wrote to Patmore about this new work in a letter that was later included in the *Liber Amoris*: 'On the road down I began a little book of our conversations, i.e. mine and the statue's. You shall see it when I come back.'

His love affair with Sarah had been intermittently finding its way into his writing for over a year. But by March

1822 Hazlitt had definitely conceived the idea that, whatever other outcome his love affair with Sarah might have, he would turn his passion into a book. Initially written as a series of semi-dramatised lovers' dialogues it would over the coming months develop into a more subtle and complex work.

He had also found another identity for Sarah, the 'statue', that was increasingly to preoccupy him. Like a statue she seemed cold and indifferent to him but, like the little statue of Napoleon, she was also a figure that he idolised.

Hazlitt wrote to Patmore from Renton Inn, located about 40 miles east of Edinburgh. Before he moved there, Hazlitt had spent a week in the city, preparing evidence of the adultery that his wife would use in their divorce proceedings. Hazlitt was guided in these arrangements by a lawyer, Alexander Henderson, who had directed him to a brothel on James Street in the port town of Leith, a few miles from the main city of Edinburgh. Hazlitt arranged to be discovered with Mary Walker, a woman who worked there.

Once Hazlitt had set up this masquerade he left for the peace of Renton Inn. Edinburgh was an uneasy city for him. Francis Jeffrey, editor of the *Edinburgh Review*, lived there. Jeffrey was one of the few editors Hazlitt genuinely admired and he found him a sympathetic host during the early days of his stay in Edinburgh. But Edinburgh was also home to some of Hazlitt's fiercest critics, including *Blackwood's*, the magazine that had conducted the most sustained attack on his reputation. If the news got around that he was in Edinburgh they would want to know why, and Hazlitt did not want his divorce to become fresh material for attack. There were other reasons for withdrawing from town. Hazlitt wanted solitude in order to write and think about the absent Sarah.

Alone in Renton Inn, Hazlitt started work on a new series of *Table Talk* essays. Over the next four weeks, he contined writing at a prodigious rate. In early March he wrote to Patmore listing what he had written: nine essays, each about 10,000 words in length.

Hazlitt's work rate was one sign of his continued determination to redefine himself as a writer. He still wanted to explore the potentials of his chosen form, the 'original essay'. But his literary ambition now also became a part of his ambitions as a lover. Writing essays at Renton Inn may have kept loneliness at bay; it was a way of conducting conversations with himself when nobody else was around to reply. But his industry was also a sign of his virtue and prudence as a potential husband. It was a way of impressing Sarah without frightening her, something he tried to make clear in a letter he sent to her in February:

> You will scold me for this, and ask me if this is keeping my promise to mind my work. One half of it was to think of Sarah; and besides I do not neglect my work either, I assure you. I regularly do ten pages a day, which mounts up to thirty guineas worth a week. And I could keep on so, if I had you with me to encourage me with your sweet smiles and share my lot...

He begins by sounding like a little boy, 'a child in love', who wants praise for finishing his homework. He can write his pages, do his sums, and plan for the future. But this picture of industry needs something to make it complete: the wife who will encourage and sustain the literary effort needed to make a comfortable living; hence the turn in the letter to a forlorn kind of cajoling, and what is virtually a proposal of marriage.

These vulnerable hopes were not the only results of Hazlitt's solitude. Something darker and more depressed was at work in him too. In the rest of his letter to Sarah, he veers from imagining a future for them to thinking about a very different kind of union – one where he will creep back to her when both are old, and she is without a partner, only to die in her arms. Their relationship ceases to have a life in the present and is postponed to an impossible future or consigned to the past:

> You once made me believe I was not hated by her I loved; and for that sensation, so delicious was it, though but a mockery and a dream, I owe you more than I can ever pay...

These words try to make a gift out of deprivation. Hazlitt acknowledges that he is quite probably deluded about Sarah's love for him, but is prepared to pay that price for what the delusion allows him to feel – not being hated by someone he loves.

Hazlitt is moved to tears by the power of his own words to describe his condition. They bring to life again the grief he felt when he left Sarah to go to Scotland:

> I thought to have dried up my tears for ever, the day I left you: but as I write this, they stream again. If they did not I think my heart would burst...

This sad self-portrait – and the tearful appeal for love it contains – is carried along by a familiar ambivalence in Hazlitt's mood: his tendency, within the space of a few sentences, to move from imagining a future with Sarah to believing that it was all over between them.

One essay he wrote during his stay at Renton Inn, *On the Knowledge of Character*, gives a further indication of the fluctuations in his mood. In it he declared his belief in love at first sight and rhapsodically addressed Sarah, although not directly by name, as 'thou, who the first time I ever beheld thee, didst draw my soul into the circle of thy heavenly looks... do not think thy conquest less complete because it was instantaneous'.

But Hazlitt was still engaged in an argument with himself about whether writers could be lovers. A few sentences before his words of love he had been doubting this ability: 'An argument immediately draws off the schol- ar's attention from the prettiest woman in the room.'

His self-consciousness was such that he could readily find a description for his behaviour with Sarah that made it seem as if he was simply playing the wrong part in the wrong play. He says as much in long letter to his son in which he offers some fatherly advice on how to prosper in the world.

To make letters like this public was not unusual and Hazlitt decided to do this for the Paris edition of his *Table Talk* essays published in 1825. What didn't appear in the published text but did in the original letter indicates his deep pessimism about his love affair with Sarah, or any other woman. He stoically presents his own life to his son as a list of errors to be avoided. He returns emphatically to the dangers of women in books. Literary accounts of love encourage sentimentality and idealism:

> All your fine sentiments and romantic notions will (of themselves) make no more impression on one of these delicate creatures than on a piece of marble. Their soft bosoms are steel to your amorous refinements, if you have no other pretensions. It is not what you think of them that determines their choice, but what they think of you... if a woman does not like you of her own accord, that is, from involuntary impressions, nothing you can say or do or suffer for her sake will make her...

A palpable experience of rejection lies just on the other side of these sentences, as does the bitter suspicious wisdom that comes from it. Hazlitt warns against two fatal illusions in love: one, that because you love somebody they will love you in return, and, secondly, that telling someone you love them will conjure love from them. Women may look soft and enticing, but words alone, however well meant, can have little effect.

Authors are especially prone to errors in love because of the work they do. The 'pretensions' they lack include the 'dress and address' necessary to social and sexual success. Women, Hazlitt advises his son, 'care nothing about poets, philosophers, or politicians. They go by a man's looks and manner... The natural and instinctive pattern of love is excited by qualities not peculiar to artists, authors and men of letters'. And, as far as authors are concerned, their profession alienates them from this 'natural and instinctive pattern':

> Authors... feel nothing spontaneously... Nothing stirs in their blood or accelerates their juices or tickles their veins. Instead of yielding to the first natural and lively impulse of things, in which they would find sympathy, they screw themselves up to some far-fetched view of the subject in order to be intelligible...

In this letter, Hazlitt repeats with renewed conviction the opinions on authors and love he had written about in his 1815 essay, *On the Literary Character*. Authors were always watching their feelings to see how they could be worked up into memorable words. Love, or any other emotion, was not valuable for its own sake. It was all potential material. He was still haunted by the feeling that writing about love destroyed the possibility of real love in one's life.

Another thing haunted him: the thought of his utter loneliness and failure. What started out as a letter of advice comes close to a self-analysis that combines self-pity and self-loathing in equal measure:

A spider, my dear, the meanest creature that crawls or lives, has its mate or fellow: but a scholar has no mate or fellow. For myself, I had courted thought, I had felt pain; and Love turned his face from me. I have gazed along the silent air for that smile which lured me to my doom. I no more heard those accents, which would have burst upon me, like a voice from heaven. I loathed the light that shone on my disgrace...

Writing about his divided feelings for Sarah became a way of working them up into a tormenting dance. At one moment his words could lead him to a dream of happiness, at another into a bitter analysis of his own delusion.

In effect, and perhaps without knowing it, he was behaving like his favourite actor, Edmund Kean, who had impressed audiences with his intense and emotionally explosive presence on stage. Hazlitt had been Kean's advocate and celebrated a new style of Romantic acting he brought to the English theatre. The 'rapidity of his transitions from one tone or feeling to another' and 'the conflicts of passion arising out of conflicts in situation' that Hazlitt admired in Kean's performance of Shylock found an echo in the way he lived out his own emotions. Kean created a style that he came to imitate. Indeed Patmore had noticed a similarity between the two men. He thought Hazlitt's 'mouth greatly resembled Edmund Kean's, the eyes grey (furtive), sometimes sinister'.

Rapid transitions certainly characterised Hazlitt's mood in the days after he finished his letter to his son. On March 5th, he wrote to Patmore and then, a few days later, to Sarah.

In the first letter he plays the part of the cynical libertine, in the second he becomes the devoted lover. To

Patmore he calls Sarah 'little Yes and No'. As evidence of her caprice he included a letter from Sarah in the letter he sent to Patmore. Her words, formal and restrained as usual, become an occasion for Hazlitt's commentary. Her coolness to him is a sign of duplicity. He suspects her of carrying on with someone else. She is probably a whore – 'an arrant jilt' is the phrase Hazlitt uses – but he still loves her. Whatever proposals he makes to her she refuses to respond to directly.

Yet all the time something else is playing through this commentary: Hazlitt's recollection of his conversations with Sarah the night before he left for Edinburgh. The form of the 'little book of our conversations', begun in Renton, surfaces briefly in this letter to Patmore, and the voices of the two lovers, one questioning, the other hesitating, suggest a sadder reality than Hazlitt wants to claim:

H. Could you not come and live with me, as a friend, a sister?
S. I don't know: & yet it would be of no use if I did, you would always be hankering after what could never be.

Hazlitt's recollection of Sarah's words indicates a

possibility that he wants to ignore. She was simply being as straightforward with him as she could be, rejecting his hopes for their life together.

In his letter to Sarah, he begins with a mild reproach for the brevity and detachment of her letters – 'You are such a girl for business' – but goes on rapidly to reassure her that he could never send her an 'unkind word', or 'do aught to cast the slightest blame upon thee'. Unkind words and blame were clearly reserved for his letters to Patmore.

He goes on to entertain her with stories about the servants at Renton Inn, before changing the subject again to recall 'that delicious night I saw *Romeo and Juliet* with you and your sweet mother'. In his recollection Sarah is not the 'arrant jilt' or the 'sweet bitch' of the letter to Patmore, but an emblem of feminine decorum:

> Can I ever forget it for a moment – your sweet modest looks, your infinite propriety of behaviour, all your sweet ways... your stepping into the coach without my being able to make an inch of discovery.

The sweetness of Sarah's modesty lies in the eroticism it hints at but discreetly veils. In his recollection of the evening Hazlitt is delighted to be denied and ready to live off the memory of their holding hands or his contemplation of her face.

But Hazlitt writes to Sarah as if trying to delay the rejection that he knows he risks. He wants to lead her away from memories of rows and emotional damage to something more innocent. He wants her to keep a picture of him as a child, painted by his brother. His adult face, marked by what he calls his 'bad passions' rather than his 'good feelings', can be restored by her love to its child-like state. Everything good remains possible if only she will love him.

CHAPTER SIX
DELAY

By the middle of March Hazlitt had completed the 40 days of residence in Scotland that were required by Scottish law. He had also finished work on his *Table Talk* essays and sent the volume off to his London publisher, Henry Colbourn. He left Renton Inn for Edinburgh, hoping to meet his wife there.

But Sarah Hazlitt did not arrive when Hazlitt hoped she would. She had decided to spend time with her son while he was on holiday from Dawson's Academy. Whatever her feelings about going through with the divorce, she could be in no doubt about the opposition from Hazlitt's family. In late March, Hazlitt's mother and sister sent her a sympathetic letter. Grace, Hazlitt's mother, was distressed by the behaviour of both her sons. John, her oldest son and a portrait painter, was by this stage in his life an alcoholic. Her other son, William, was now intent on divorcing his wife in pursuit of what seemed to her a scandalous affair. Peggy, Hazlitt's sister, was more vehement still. She thought her brother was mad and hoped that Sarah would not be persuaded to go to Scotland. She was also concerned that their letter might get into the wrong hands, giving publicity to Hazlitt's behaviour and so shaming the family or making him aware of what she really thought. At the end of her letter she advised Sarah to burn it.

While Sarah stayed in England, her husband grew increasingly agitated in Edinburgh. He waited on his wife's arrival. He waited on a letter from Sarah Walker. Neither came. He visited Francis Jeffrey, the editor of the *Edinburgh Review*, feeling 'dull and out of spirits'. Jeffrey assured him that it didn't show, but this gave Hazlitt scant consolation. The whole project of the divorce from his wife and the proposal of marriage to Sarah seemed to be foundering. A letter from Patmore sent to Hazlitt sometime in March made him more miserable still. The text of the letter from Patmore doesn't survive, but it must have contained some news about Sarah that renewed Hazlitt's jealousy. His letter to Patmore, written on March 30th, is haunted with a desire for oblivion. His efforts to interpret Sarah's silence lead him back to the intolerable thought that its cause is her love for another man:

> Can you account for it except on the admission of my worst suspicion that she has... Oh! my God! Can I bear to think of her so, or that I am scorned and made sport of by the creature to whom I had given my very heart? I feel like one of the damned.

Having seemed to promise the love that Hazlitt had never experienced, Sarah now threatened to confirm his own worst fantasy: 'To be hated, loathed as I have been all my life, and to feel the utter impossibility of its ever being otherwise while I live — take what pains I may!' The way out of this torment is not suicide — Hazlitt admits that he is too much of a coward for that — but another kind of oblivion. He craves a state of emotional and mental passivity, 'to be an ideot for some few years and then wake up a poor wretched old man, to recollect my misery as past, and die'. The one consolation in his life would be to know that it's over.

The shape of this letter to Patmore suggests that writing in this way still held some therapeutic value for Hazlitt.

He dives into his misery, swirls in its depths, and then surfaces again. The letter ends in the everyday world of plans
and work. Hazlitt tells Patmore that he has finished his
book of conversations with Sarah. The work now has a
title, *Liber Amoris*.

In fact Hazlitt was to spend the coming months rewrit-
ing and expanding the book. Perhaps he was now driven by
a new motive. He would pursue his passion for Sarah
because he wanted to turn it into a book. He would treat
his own life and hers as material for a literary experiment.
In a concluding sentence he ironically recommends the
book that is taking shape as a piece of 'very nice reading'.

Irony proved a fragile defence against the workings
of Hazlitt's imagination. His vexed state at the end of
March and beginning of April showed in his movements
back and forth between Renton Inn and Edinburgh. He
had received the proofs for the second volume of *Table Talk*
which was planned for publication in June. It was probably
at this stage that he chose to add a passage to his essay,
On the Knowledge of Character, that he had written during
his February stay at Renton Inn. If Sarah had appeared
anonymously in the first draft of that essay as 'that gentle
form… all that I had ever loved of female grace, modesty,
and sweetness', she now made another anonymous

appearance in a different guise:

> The greatest hypocrite I ever knew was a little, demure, pretty, modest-looking girl with eyes timidly cast upon the ground and an air soft as enchantment; the only circumstance that could lead to suspicion of her true character was a cold, sullen, watery, glazed look about the eyes, which she bent on vacancy, as if determined to avoid all explanation with yours. I might have spied in their glittering, motionless surface, the rocks and quicksands that awaited me below!

The published essay is presented in a way that allows the reader to assume that the 'hypocrite' and the 'gentle form' are two different women. But Hazlitt was thinking of only one. 'Female grace' has suddenly been reimagined as a 'cold, sullen watery, glazed look about the eyes'. Sarah is not just to be doubted but dismissed. Hazlitt's regret here is not for a love that has been lost but for a mistake that he should have seen coming.

In early April, Patmore wrote a letter to Hazlitt trying to reassure him about Sarah. Hazlitt's reply of April 7th, 1822, suggested that he didn't find Patmore's words particularly convincing. He took some comfort from the news that his wife had decided on the date for her journey to Scotland. But, isolated in Edinburgh, Hazlitt tied himself in jealous knots:

> What security can I have that she does not flirt or worse with everyone that comes in her way when I recollect how she took my first advances?... And what can I think of a girl who grants a man she has no particle of regard for the freedoms she has done to me?...

He wanted Patmore to help him break Sarah's silence, but was like a script-writer who couldn't work out what story he should tell. He wanted to know what was going on in Southampton Buildings and then decided that he couldn't bear to find out. A proposal that Patmore should visit Sarah to encourage her to write to Hazlitt was countermanded by a couple of sentences written across the top of the letter's first page:

> FINAL. Don't go at all. I believe her to be a common lodging-house drab, and that any attempt only hardens her.

No other letter to Patmore moves with such speed between his two images of Sarah, the sweet angel and the lascivious whore. Sentences have been scored through in heavy black ink. It is not clear who has done this or who has made the subsequent efforts to restore what has been deleted. The deletions may have been made by Hazlitt's son, concerned that preserving the letter in its uncut form might damage his father's reputation. Richard le Galliene, a late-nineteenth-century decadent poet, may be the source of the restorations. He published an edition of *Liber Amoris* and Hazlitt's letters about Sarah in 1894. Where Hazlitt's son felt that the letter disclosed a shameful and offensive secret, le Galliene clearly saw it as a fascinating document in human psychology.

One of the passages is dominated by Hazlitt's leering portrait of Sarah as a sexual tease. She uses men to gratify her desire and avoid pregnancy:

> All she wants is to be tickled and go all lengths but the last to be thrown on the floor and felt and all and still resist and keep up the game. To think that I should feel as I have done for such a monster.

Hazlitt imagines himself here as a man of sensibility

who has wasted his fine feelings on an egotistical and inhuman pleasure seeker. But in an earlier passage he had remembered Sarah longingly 'in her morning gown, in her dirt, and her mob cap', leading him to a memory of their caresses:

> ...it is so she has oftenest sat on my knee with her arms around my neck – Damn her, I could devour her, it is herself that I love.

The letter then becomes increasingly confused. Two lines are deleted and partially restored. What has been restored seems to allude back to one of Hazlitt's earlier sexual encounters, 'I went with a girl that was what they call – and fancied she was 15,' and then the letter resumes with the following disjointed sentence: 'and though it's what I hate, I adored her the more for it.'

The letter is, at this point, a tissue of enigmas and yet it seems to point to something important and disturbed both in Hazlitt's sexual history and in his relation to Sarah. We cannot know exactly what 'they' called the girl who Hazlitt fancied was fifteen. Perhaps she was called a 'virgin'. We can assume that it is something about Sarah that he hates and adores, or some similarity between Sarah and the unnamed girl.

One key to these enigmas may lie in an issue that dominates Hazlitt's letter to Patmore: the significance of Sarah's refusal to let Hazlitt have genital sex with her. In one vision of her, this is what made her monstrous. She was having sex with other men while denying it to him. But, in another, it's what made her sweet and nymph-like, a creature poised between being a virginal girl and a sensuous woman. She enticed him and then refused him. Her refusal made him want her more. What stood in the way of his desire also intensified it.

For Hazlitt, the double bind – that what made Sarah delightful could also make her monstrous – grew out of the most intimate moments of their relationship. Her continuing silence only intensified his sense that he was encountering something outside his control.

We can't know exactly why she kept quiet. She may have been angered discovering that Hazlitt had been showing her letters to Patmore or vexed by his use of Patmore as a go-between. Nor was he the only one involved. Before he left for Edinburgh, Hazlitt had visited Sarah's aunt to ask for her help in discovering Sarah's true feelings. She had found this out while Hazlitt was away. His willingness to draw others into their relationship irritated her. It was just one more sign of his insistence that she was under some obligation to respond to him. Or her silence may have had another source. If her relationship with Tomkins was important to her then his departure from Southampton Buildings in March may have raised a question mark in her mind over its future.

One further clue is given by an entry in the journal that Hazlitt's wife kept during her stay in Scotland between April and July 1822. The entry, for July 17th, records a long conversation with her husband, most of it about his passion for Sarah Walker. At one point in the conversation Sarah Hazlitt remarks to him that 'he had done a most injudicious thing in publishing what he had done in the Magazine about Sarah Walker… and that he might be sure it would be made use of against him, and that everybody in London had thought he had done a most improper thing'. Hazlitt acknowledged that 'it had hurt the girl too, and done her an injury'.

The 'most improper thing' was an essay, *On Great and Little Things*, published in the *New Monthly Magazine* in February 1822. Hazlitt's usual practice as a writer was to treat the proofs of his essays and articles as a stage in the process of composition. It was an opportunity for him to make revisions, additions and deletions. But, in the case of this essay, Henry Colbourn, Hazlitt's publisher, had not sent him any proofs. The procedure that had allowed Hazlitt to cut references to his passion in *The Fight* had not worked here.

On Great and Little Things is an extended meditation on an apparent puzzle in human behaviour: the tendency to be provoked into irritation and anger by relatively trivial things while calmly accepting major disasters. Hazlitt's explanation for this puzzle is that we are more provoked by slight setbacks because we believe we could have prevented them. Disasters, on the other hand, happen as a result of forces beyond our control. This leads into a reflection on different kinds of discrepancy in human life. One example Hazlitt uses of a damaging difference between people is the 'misery of unequal matches', which, in his case, means marriages where the wife comes from a lower social class than the husband.

The example is the opening for Sarah Walker's entry into his essay. Under her pseudonym, Infelice, she once again will be the exception that proves the rule and the essay becomes more personal in tone:

But shouldst thou ever, my Infelice, grace my home with thy loved presence, as thou hast cheered my hopes with thy smile, thou wilt conquer all hearts with thy prevailing gentleness, and I will shew the world what Shakespear's women were!

These words, and others like them, did not go down well. Hazlitt acknowledged to his wife that they had hurt Sarah Walker; indeed he seems to have anticipated that lines like these would cause trouble. After a long passage about love in the essay – one that included this address to Infelice – he added a footnote: 'I beg the reader to consider this passage merely a specimen of the mock-heroic style, and as having nothing to do with real facts and feelings.' This reads like a hasty and defensive afterthought. Real facts and feelings were involved. Hazlitt must have known that at least some of his readers knew that Sarah Walker was the woman he was asking to redeem his life. Sarah Hazlitt had no doubt that Hazlitt's enemies knew about Sarah Walker as well. Putting his passion into print, even inadvertently, was courting trouble for both of them.

Whatever Sarah Walker knew or didn't know, whatever she was doing or not doing, Hazlitt's actions as a writer were not helping his cause as a lover. Her silence continued. Patmore carried on in his role of mediator. He responded to Hazlitt's turbulent letters by challenging his description of Sarah as a 'common lodging-house drab', defending her against the corrosive force of his jealousy.

On April 21st, Hazlitt wrote to Patmore in a calmer and more optimistic mood. He was prepared to accept Patmore's rebuke. He was also cheered by the news that Sarah Hazlitt had just arrived in Edinburgh. But as much as anything else he was pleased by a piece of verbal play that helped him to reimagine Sarah. Hazlitt and Patmore had been trading quotations in their letters from Shakespeare's tragedy of sexual jealousy, *Othello*. The play's story provided Hazlitt with a reference point for his own broodings on Sarah Walker. In his letter to Hazlitt, Patmore reversed the sense of some of Iago's lines in the original. Iago works on Othello by encouraging him to believe that it is normal for all women to be unfaithful. It is common 'To lip a wanton in a secure couch/And to suppose her chaste'. Patmore changes the lines to persuade Hazlitt that his mistake is the opposite, and Hazlitt thanks him for it:

She is my soul's idol, and believe me those words of yours applied to the dear creature, 'To lip a chaste one and suppose her wanton' were balm and rapture to me.

Changing a few words seemed to change the world for Hazlitt. With the 'balm and rapture' of what Patmore had written inside him, Hazlitt was drawn back to an idea that had seemed impossible only a few weeks earlier — that Sarah might after all be able to marry him:

> When I sometimes think of the time I first saw the sweet apparition, August 16th 1820, and that perhaps possibly she may be my wife before that day two years, it makes me mad with incredible joy and love of her.

CHAPTER SEVEN
THE WIFE

Sarah Hazlitt was a writer, too, but of a very different kind to her husband. During her three-month stay in Scotland she kept a journal that provides a record of the legal process of her divorce, her occasional conversations with her husband, and her travels in Scotland and Ireland while she waited on her appearances in court. Unlike her husband, Sarah did not intend her work for publication. The tone of her journal is quiet and dispassionate. It provides some insight into her mental and emotional state at the time and also shows how frankly the Hazlitts talked to each other about what was happening between them.

One thing the journal makes clear is that Sarah had no religious or ethical objections to the divorce. Nor did she want to play the part of an abandoned wife. Sarah was an outspoken, free-spirited and well-read woman, who, like her husband, was prepared to live an unconventional life. Hazlitt had first met her in 1807. She was sexually experienced and a source of worry to her older brother, John Stoddart, who was by then her legal guardian. Earlier, in 1797, he had written to Sarah telling her that she was 'deficient in those minutiae of taste and conduct which constitute elegance of manners and mental refinement'. This pompous concern for his younger sister did not have much effect on her behaviour. When she and Hazlitt married in 1808, John Stoddart did not approve of the match. He was by then a senior journalist on *The Times* and disliked Hazlitt's politics. The couple managed to win him over temporarily, but it wasn't long before his disapproval of Hazlitt led to a permanent break between them.

Three things concerned Sarah about her divorce: the law, money and her son. Within a day of her arrival in Edinburgh, she met with George Cranstoun, an experienced and respected barrister who had agreed to represent her. She was accompanied at this meeting by John Robertson Bell, a failed businessman, who had met the Hazlitts when they lived in London in 1815. Bell presented himself as the honest broker in the divorce, someone who was willing to help both husband and wife through the difficulties they both faced. It was Bell who told Hazlitt of his wife's arrival in Edinburgh and Hazlitt, initially at least, assumed that he was the right person to help.

Sarah's first meeting with Cranstoun was dominated by her concerns about the Oath of Calumny. She knew she was running the risk of deportation for perjury if there was evidence that she and her husband had colluded in setting up the divorce. To Sarah it seemed obvious that they had. Hazlitt had made clear to her before going to Scotland that he no longer wanted to live with her. He told her that a divorce was in both their interests and Sarah had not disagreed with him. Cranstoun tried to reassure her. Hazlitt had repeatedly committed adultery during their marriage. She had not colluded with him then. His being discovered in an adulterous affair in Scotland was part of a pattern. It was not likely to be viewed as the result of a deliberate agreement between them to end their marriage.

But Cranstoun was conscious of the fact that he was giving an opinion, not a definitive judgement. He recommended a further consultation, this time with a solicitor, John Gray, who would be needed as a source of advice and, according to legal requirement, as an intermediary between Sarah and Cranstoun. She met with Gray on April

23rd and discussed the legal process with him. He had to identify the name and address of the woman Hazlitt had arranged to be discovered with. Then Sarah had to put forward a complaint against her husband. Then they had to wait to see if the complaint was admitted and Sarah allowed to take the Oath of Calumny. If each step went according to plan the divorce would be finalised in a couple of months.

The law laid bare in dry and solemn language the failure of the Hazlitts' marriage. Within a few days of their first meeting Gray supplied Sarah with a text of her complaint against her husband. It alleged frequent adulteries in 'the City of London and suburbs thereof, and in the City of Edinburgh and Suburbs thereof...' It included the more specific allegation that Hazlitt 'had carnal and adulterous intercourse and dealings with a woman of the name Mary Walker in a house in James Street, Edinburgh'.

Her initial consultations with Gray did not give Sarah the further assurance she needed. She discovered that the wording of the Oath of Calumny proposed by Gray did not correspond to a version she had discovered in an authoritative legal text, Robert Boyd's *Judicial Proceedings*. Sarah did not want simply to accept the legal advice she was given. On April 25th she sent a note to Hazlitt telling him that she 'demurred the Oath'. This was a legal move on her part. A demurral assumed the truth of Hazlitt's adulteries, but also indicated that the evidence was not strong enough to protect Sarah against an accusation of collusion. She also wanted to ensure that Hazlitt was going to do what he had promised to do in going through with the divorce. She drew up a memorandum for him to sign that set out his agreement to pay for the costs of the divorce, her stay in Scotland, and the future costs of their son's education, as well as a guarantee of her access to the boy as and when she decided.

Hazlitt's hopes for a quick resolution of his divorce rapidly faded. He became increasingly agitated about the obstacles that stood in the way of his plan to go down to London and propose marriage to Sarah Walker. On the same day that Sarah sent her note demurring the Oath, William Ritchie – an editor of the recently founded paper, the *Scotsman*, and a sympathetic friend to Hazlitt while he was in Edinburgh – visited her at her lodgings in South Union Place. He wanted to persuade her to go ahead with the divorce, and combined flattery and emotional blackmail to get her to agree. According to Sarah's journal, he told her that she was still attractive and would easily find another husband. As for Hazlitt, Ritchie told Sarah that he was 'in a state of nervous irritability that he could not work or apply to anything and that he thought he would not live very long if he was not easier in his mind'.

The Hazlitts' divorce was like a rickety machine, hard to get going and difficult to control once started. One step forward was followed by two steps backward. To get the proceedings underway Hazlitt had been formally identified on April 25th as the person who had been caught *in flagrante delicto* with a woman in her room at a lodging house or brothel in 21 James Street. But Mrs. Knight, who ran the house, was becoming increasingly anxious that her reputation and livelihood would be threatened if she or her lodgings were mentioned in the divorce proceedings.

Meanwhile, Sarah Hazlitt's worries about money did not go away. Hazlitt had agreed to pay for her stay in Scotland. By the end of April she had spent most of the money she had brought with her and threatened to return to London if her husband did not meet his side of the bargain. He, in turn, would only agree to give her more money if she agreed to take the Oath of Calumny. Messages went back and forth but without a resolution. As a diversion from the pressure, Sarah went sightseeing in Edinburgh and Hazlitt himself set out for Lanark. He wanted to write an article about the model community established there by the industrialist and social reformer Robert Owen. Nothing came of the project and Hazlitt returned to Edinburgh on April 30th.

On the evening of the same day, Sarah took the risky step of talking to her husband face to face. If they were seen talking together this might be used against them as evidence of collusion. She went to his lodgings in George Street, wearing a veil to avoid detection. Her journal entry for that day provides a detailed account of their conversation. Sarah was clearly intent on documenting what was said, not analysing it, but the topics of their conversation and its resolution give an insight into what sustained their marriage and what broke it apart.

Sarah's main motive in making the visit was to sort out her financial situation. She had written to Hazlitt on April 28th to tell him that she was running out of money.

Hazlitt promised to pay what they had agreed. But, as in most of his financial dealings, the money he was pledging had not yet arrived. He expected money from his publisher, Colbourn, and had agreed to give a couple of lectures in Glasgow which he thought would bring him a further £100. He was due another £80 in part payment for the second volume of *Table Talk*, due to be published in June. His promises turned to sarcasm when he suggested that, in addition to what had been agreed, he would give Sarah another £20 as a 'handsome present' because she seemed 'to love money'. Sarah clearly resented this and insisted that her main purpose was to ensure that the costs of their son's education were met. Hazlitt replied that if she did not agree to the divorce he would leave the country and refuse any further financial responsibilities.

One accusation led to another. The couple were now in the familiar mode of a marital row. Accusations about small things raised larger questions about their trust in each other and their care for their son. Recriminations about his education led to the wider question of his upbringing. Hazlitt tried to defend his record as a father. He didn't need Sarah to remind him of his responsibilities nor of his devotion to his son. Sarah did not deny that he was a kind father, but doubted his ability to provide a secure framework for their son's future. She questioned the consequences of his kindness if it led to young William accompanying his father when Hazlitt 'went picking up girls on the town'. Behind this remark Hazlitt detected evidence of Sarah trying to turn their son against him. Sarah denied it. Mention of 'girls on the town' provoked Hazlitt's anxiety about what women thought of him. The question of his 'abilities' and how these were perceived by women surfaced again. Hazlitt claimed that Sarah had always despised him. She refused to rise to this bait and responded by asking Hazlitt what he imagined the girls he picked up thought of his literary talents. She shrewdly observed that Hazlitt's desire for anonymity and his wish to be with women who did not know he was an author with a public reputation were a sign of his intense sensitivity about how others regarded him. 'Nobody', as she put it, 'was more sore on that point.' In his memoirs, Patmore described a similar sensitivity. Hazlitt thought hostile reviews turned the world against him:

> ...if he entered a coffee house where he was known to get his dinner, it was impossible (he thought) that the waiters would be doing anything else all the time he was there, but pointing him out to guests as 'the gentleman who was so abused last month in BM [*Blackwood's Magazine*]'.

Perhaps the couple were repeating an argument they had had before. But there was a difference this time. They both finally agreed to end their marriage but it is indicative of the respect they had for each other that they both ultimately held back from real acrimony. Nothing definite was agreed between them, but neither wanted to destroy the other. Sarah anticipated an end of all contact between them. Hazlitt replied that, once the divorce was finalised, he hoped that they could remain good friends.

Their conversation brought with it the realisation that they would have to cooperate in order to separate. Within a few days, Hazlitt had signed the memorandum agreeing to Sarah's terms and she had received some money, although not as much as she had initially been promised. Sarah agreed to take the Oath of Calumny. John Gray went to the brothel in James Street, brought some of the regulars there the drink that they demanded and got the information he needed about Hazlitt's visits to Mary Walker. By May 3rd, Sarah's complaint alleging adultery had been served on Hazlitt. The law gave Hazlitt fifteen days to consider his response. The Commissioners charged with judging the case would expect him to take his time and they, in turn, would need a week to consider Hazlitt's reply. Once again the process of law required the couple to move at its pace. No further progress with the divorce was possible for another three weeks.

Sarah decided to leave Edinburgh and go on a walking tour of Scotland. Hazlitt went over to Glasgow to give two lectures at the Andersonian Insititute. He had been invited there by James Sheridan Knowles, a successful playwright and the owner of a newspaper, the *Glasgow Free Press*. The two men had known each other for a long time. Hazlitt, in his early and unsuccessful attempt to become a painter, had started a portrait of Knowles in 1799. In May 1820, Hazlitt had praised Knowles's play, *Virginius*, when it was first shown in Covent Garden. In his drama column he hailed it as 'a real tragedy; a sound historical painting'. Knowles, another of Hazlitt's young admirers, found Hazlitt sympathetic and thought him misunderstood. He wanted to help his friend at a difficult moment. The fee for the lectures would go some way to helping Hazlitt meet the costs of his divorce.

Hazlitt gave his first lecture on May 6th and the second on May 13th. His presence in Glasgow and the content of his lectures were reported in the local press. Reactions split along predictable political lines. Other things, though, were on his mind. Sheridan Knowles went with him on a walking tour to Loch Lomond. Their conversation was mostly about Sarah Walker and his impending divorce. Whatever was said did little to calm Hazlitt's nerves.

He could not endure his separation from Sarah any longer and on May 14th he left Glasgow for Edinburgh.

From there he booked a passage on a boat to London. It arrived at Blackwall docks on the 17th. 'The air', as Hazlitt later described it, 'thickened with the consciousness of being near her.'

CHAPTER EIGHT
THE RETURN

Sarah met Hazlitt in his old rooms at Southampton Buildings. She was taciturn and withdrawn. He coaxed, cajoled and questioned her. Her brief replies gave him little reassurance. Her feelings had not changed while he had been away; there was no rival for her affections; she had not replied to his letters because she didn't think they required a reply. Their first meeting did not last long. It gave Hazlitt little cause for hope.

The uneasy stand-off between them continued the following day. Sarah kept her distance. She did not serve Hazlitt breakfast as he hoped she would, but he took some reassurance at the sight of the little statue of Napoleon on the mantelpiece in his sitting room. He took it as a sign

that Sarah had remembered its significance to both of them
and had made sure that it was in its usual place. On Sunday
her mood seemed to soften. She handed Hazlitt the newspaper when he came down from his rooms in search of
it. Feeding off scraps again, Hazlitt interpreted this as an
affectionate gesture. He had arranged to meet his son that
morning and the two of them went for a walk. It is clear
from the account that Hazlitt gave in *Liber Amoris* that his
son, William, had already met Sarah and that there had
been a disagreement between them. Hazlitt persuaded
William to return with him to Southampton Buildings and
apologise.

Sarah responded to William's apology generously: she
did not want to harbour grudges and shook hands with
him. Hazlitt took this as an opportunity to remind her of
his feelings for her by way of a conversation about the
little statue:

'I see you brought me back my little Buonaparte'—
She answered with tremulous softness – 'I told you
I'd keep it safe for you'... I was delighted with the
alteration in her manner, and said, referring to the
bust – 'You know it's not mine, but your's; I gave
it you; nay, I have given you all my heart, and

whatever I possess, is your's!' She seemed good-humouredly to decline this carte blanche offer, and waved, like a thing of enchantment, out of the room.

Hazlitt still had not succeeded in having the conversation he craved. He tried to renew contact with her that evening when William had gone, again using the 'little image' as a pretext, but she would only agree to talk across the threshold of Hazlitt's sitting-room door. He sat on a chair on one side of it, close enough to hold her hand. She stood and listened as Hazlitt repeated the story of his passion for her. She would not give him the words he wanted in return. She insisted that her feelings for him were unchanged, but that they were feelings of friendship not love. Hazlitt tried to persuade himself that her resistance was still due to the fact that he was not yet in a position to propose marriage. He grew more intense as she grew more dispassionate. He asked her for a kiss and, according to Hazlitt's account, she refused him for the first time, then turned away and walked down the stairs towards the ground-floor rooms she shared with her family.

Hazlitt was overwhelmed with grief and rage. He tore the locket of Sarah's hair from his neck and trampled on it.

He took the little statue of Napoleon from the mantel-piece, hurled it on the ground, and crushed it underfoot. There seemed nothing more he could do to persuade Sarah to love him. His situation had become intolerable:

> I could not stay in the room; I could not leave it; my rage and despair were uncontrollable. I shrieked curses on her name, and on her false love; and the scream I uttered (so pitiful and piercing was it that the sound of it terrified me) instantly brought the whole house, father, mother, lodgers and all, into the room.

The inhabitants of Southampton Buildings may have thought he was threatening violence to Sarah, believing his scream to be hers. What they discovered was a very different scene.

Hazlitt was now without a hiding place or home. The lodging house had become the scene of his own humiliation. He couldn't stand such exposure for long. He rushed out of his room, and into the city streets, but found being outside worse than being inside: 'the desolation and the darkness became greater, more intolerable'. What he could not bear was the thought that he and Sarah might finally have parted. He decided to go back to the lodging house.

What had looked like a terminal scene of intense passion had now turned into an uneasy comedy of unintended consequences. Hazlitt needed to explain himself, not least to Sarah's father who, in Hazlitt's own description, looked at him 'with no friendly aspect'. He did not shy away from Mr. Walker's disapproval. Instead he talked to him about his troubles with Sarah as a way of finding out how much her father knew of what had happened between them.

Their conversation established a precarious common ground. Both had been mistaken about Sarah: Mr. Walker as a father who had glimpsed Sarah sitting on Hazlitt's knee, but assumed that it was 'an accident, and that it would never happen again'; Hazlitt as a lover who thought that Sarah's caresses would be a prelude to marriage. Hazlitt wanted to make Mr. Walker an ally in his courtship of Sarah. Mr. Walker was sympathetic, but refused to put pressure on his daughter. Who she married would be her decision. Patmore had advised that Hazlitt should wait until the divorce was over before proposing marriage to Sarah. Mr. Walker agreed. Hazlitt had tried to win her over at the wrong time. He was proving again his own theory that authors were clumsy in love.

Hazlitt stayed on in Southampton Buildings until the end of May. Sarah stayed out of his way, but her sister Betsey, and her mother both acted as intermediaries, raising Hazlitt's hopes that Sarah might still care for him. He wanted to re-establish some kind of contact with her. His strategy was to make the end of the affair into a way of prolonging it. He gathered together the broken fragments of the locket and the little statue and folded them in a piece of paper. On it he wrote 'Pieces of a broken heart, to be kept in remembrance of the unhappy. Farewell.' Sarah did not respond.

Although Hazlitt wanted Sarah to know that he was planning to leave her, he resumed his habit of giving her gifts. He had given her three books that he had written. Now he asked for them back and offered three books in exchange: Goldsmith's *The Vicar of Wakefield*, Mackenzie's *The Man of Feeling*, and a translation of Goethe's *Nature and Art*, all tokens of sentiment and sensibility. Sarah refused these, just as she refused to return the books he had given her.

The episode of the books provided Hazlitt with another stimulus to his hopes. Betsey was acting as Hazlitt's go-between, moving back and forth between his sitting room and wherever Sarah was keeping out of the way. She told him that Sarah did not want to return his books because she valued them more highly than any others. This may have been a well-intentioned lie, designed to keep Hazlitt's spirits up. They were certainly the words he wanted to hear. They made him 'childish, wanton, drunk with pleasure... I murmured her name; I blest her; I folded her to my heart with delicious fondness'.

But still Sarah refused to see him. She did not come into his room with a breakfast tray. Her mother apologised for her absence. Betsey told Hazlitt that her sister was not just pleased with his books, but with *all* the books that he had given her. But living off the words of others was not enough to sustain him. He continued to crave what he had never been given: a conversation with Sarah in which they both would speak the 'language of the heart'. He continued to try and convince himself that what stood in the way of this conversation was not her unwillingness to talk to him, but some obstacle in their situation. At best that obstacle was that he was still legally married. At worst it was the presence of a rival whose existence she still denied.

Hazlitt got his wish on the evening of May 29th. Sarah agreed to an interview. She sat in his room and he kneeled before her. But Sarah did not speak the words he hoped to hear. There was no change in her mood. She repeated what she had said before, that she had no affection for him. Things had been only made worse by his behaviour the previous week. She felt shamefully exposed by what had happened. She conceded that she had been 'guilty of improprieties', but Hazlitt had only made matters worse by discussing what had happened between them with other people. The word had got back to Sarah that she was being described as a 'light creature'. She was particularly angry about a visit Hazlitt had made to Sarah's aunt to solicit her support. She had now resolved to follow her aunt's advice and 'keep every lodger at a proper distance'. Hazlitt persisted in his attempt to find the words that he believed would unlock Sarah's love, but she promised nothing, not even friendship. When Hazlitt then began to question her about the existence of a rival, she insisted that there was none. She did not want to marry. Wearied by his questions and his pleas, she again left his room.

This time Hazlitt did not cry out loud in rage and grief. He did not rush from his room out into the city streets. He experienced the world as if one of his worst fantasies about himself had come true. Sarah's departure from his room was the departure of love from his life. He was bereft. If

Adam had dreamt of Eve and woke to found it truth, Hazlitt woke to discover the opposite truth, the truth of his loneliness. He was travelling in the direction of another much more recent story, Mary Shelley's *Frankenstein*. Like the monster in Mary Shelley's story, he had been created only to be rejected:

> I started to find myself alone – for ever alone with-
> out a creature to love me. I looked round the room
> for help: I saw the tables, the chairs, the places
> where she stood or sat, empty, deserted, dead.

The life that he had hoped for had been replaced by the life that he feared. But, as so often before, Hazlitt had to find a way of talking about his state. He went downstairs and talked to Sarah's mother about what had happened. She again tried to reassure him. Her words seemed to Hazlitt to be part of a ghastly, insincere charade. Yet he felt compelled to believe what was said to him because such words still held out some hope for him. Sarah made a brief appearance while the two were talking.

To Hazlitt she seemed like an actress, pleased with the success of her deception, 'smiling with smothered delight at the consummation of my folly and her own art'. Hazlitt responded with mad gaiety. He took Mrs. Walker's 'withered, cadaverous, clammy hand', kissed it and went back upstairs to his room.

The next day, Hazlitt left Southampton Buildings and began the journey back to Edinburgh. As his steamboat travelled up the east coast of England, he wrote two letters to Patmore, the first sent from Scarborough where his boat briefly docked on May 30th, and the second from Edinburgh on the 31st. Both attempted to come to terms with Sarah's rejection. Both echo a single sentence of Sarah's, 'I always told you I had no affection for you.' The first letter responds to this sentence with romantic grief. Hazlitt has been cast out from the paradise of Sarah's love: 'I was driven from her presence, where rosy blushes and delicious sighs and all soft wishes dwelt, the outcast of nature and the scoff of love!' Like Coleridge's Ancient Mariner, he felt permanently exiled from ordinary human experience. He could not conceal his grief any longer: 'The people about me even take notice of my dumb despair, and pity me.'

The second letter is colder and harder in tone and returns to familiar territory. Sarah is a 'hardened, impudent, heartless whore'. 'She has an itch for being slabbered and felt.' She had played with Hazlitt, then with

Tomkins, and once he left the lodging house, with the Welsh apothecary Griffiths. 'The bitch wants a stallion, and hates a lover... Her addicting herself to Tomkins was endurable because he was a gentlemanly sort of fellow, but her putting up with this prick of a fellow, merely for bore and measurement and gross manners, sets me low indeed.'

Hazlitt was no longer an exile from paradise, but a fool, his manliness compromised by his failure to take Sarah sexually at their first meeting. His love for her became a kind of addiction or disease that he had to overcome. In this letter to Patmore he proposes a way of curing himself that was to preoccupy him in the coming months:

Yet if only I knew she was a whore, *flagrante delicto*, it would wean me from her, and burst my chain. Could you ascertain this fact for me, by any means or through any person... who might try her as a lodger? I should not like her to be seduced by elaborate means, but if she gave up as a matter of course, I should then be no longer the wretch I am or the God I might have been, but what I was before.

CHAPTER NINE
MADNESS

Hazlitt returned to Edinburgh just as his wife was leaving the city. After her first walking tour, Sarah Hazlitt had come back to Edinburgh on May 20th. She assumed that she would be required to take the Oath of Calumny on the 23rd. The news that her husband had gone down to London in pursuit of Sarah Walker came as a surprise. Nor had she anticipated that Hazlitt would hire a lawyer who might decide to contest her case against him, if only for the sake of appearances. One immediate result of this move was that the date for taking the Oath was postponed.

As her journal makes clear, she was irritated and upset by her husband's sudden absence. She had already spent the small sums of money Hazlitt had given her in early May. By going down to London it seemed to her that Hazlitt was ignoring their agreement to meet the expenses of her stay in Scotland. Ritchie offered to help her out, but she could only borrow money from him on the risky assumption that Hazlitt would honour this debt. Bell had turned up again with gossip about her husband and unwelcome advice. He claimed that Sarah Walker was in love with another man. He also claimed that he had seen Sarah Walker's letters and that they 'were such low, vulgar, milliners and servant wenches sentimentality that he wondered Mr. Hazlitt could endure such stuff'. Bell was making things up. The few letters to Hazlitt that Sarah Walker wrote were the opposite of sentimental. Perhaps Bell was testing Sarah Hazlitt's continuing loyalty to her husband by his remarks, finding out whether she would agree with the implied judgement that Hazlitt was acting like a fool. Sarah kept her counsel. When Bell advised her that she should move to Edinburgh and start a school for young ladies once the divorce was completed, Sarah declined his advice and ended the conversation.

Sarah Hazlitt found Edinburgh oppressive. It wasn't just that Bell talked to her about things that she didn't want to hear. His conversation was a reminder of what was happening in the city. The privacy of her marriage was exposed both to legal scrutiny and the invasions of gossip. Her husband's infidelities were becoming a matter of legal record. All this was happening not because she especially wanted it to, but because Hazlitt had convinced himself that it was vital to his future happiness.

Some of the strain she was under surfaces in her journal. On May 24th she wrote:

Very nervous and poorly today. Received a letter from Coulston to know whether I got my stamped paper and marriage certificate safe or not. Answered it. Staid at home.

Over the next few days the weather closed in; Sarah recorded in her journal for May 26th, 'very high wind and cold with hail storms and rain'. Her second stay in Edinburgh repeated a pattern evident from the time she had spent in the city earlier in the month. She often felt weak and suffered from stomach upsets. Her response was to walk as much as possible. She even walked past the brothel in James Street and caught a glimpse of 'Mrs. Knight at the window: a woman of colour with a turban on'. But walking away from Edinburgh was better than walking in it. Long walks and hard beds were easier to endure than legal complications and the city's unreliable water supply. On May 31st she crossed the Firth of Forth by boat and spent the next week travelling, mostly on foot, deep into the Highlands.

Hazlitt scarcely registered his wife's absence when he returned to Edinburgh. He couldn't stop thinking and writing about his bereft state. At the end of May he wrote a short letter to his son that mixes a queasy self-pity with a continuing willingness to make plans. He begins extravagantly, imagining a future with William, which echoes Shakespeare's *King Lear*, and the old king's fantasies about the secluded life he will lead with his daughter Cordelia:

> My dear little baby, The only comfort or tie thy poor Father has left! I send thee a pound to spend. Be happy as thou can'st my love and I will come back to thee soon, that is, before the holidays, and we will go to Winterslow Hut together and seek for peace...

As ever, Hazlitt was deeply uncertain about the form his future would take, torn between two visions. One, a life without Sarah, where his only companion would be his son. The other, more tormented, was bound up with his continuing belief that divorce would give him a future with her. Only his wife's agreement to take the Oath of Calumny could save him from madness and, in his letter to his son, Hazlitt anticipates that this will happen soon, by 'next Tuesday', June 4th. But a single mood unites these two different versions of his future. If he cannot be loved, at least he will be pitied.

In the same letter, Hazlitt gives another piece of information that may help to explain his mood. On his return to Edinburgh Jeffrey had given him £100 and not, it seems, as an advance or a loan, but as a gift, a way of helping him through a time of trouble. Pitied by all but Sarah Walker, the 'monster' who had destroyed him, Hazlitt came to think of himself as a charitable cause.

Sarah Hazlitt did not in fact take the Oath of Calumny on June 4th. She was not in Edinburgh, but walking the 22 miles from Crief to Stirling, sometimes, as her journal records, 'being overcome with heat, and not a breath of air', at others 'cut through with a strong and bleak wind'.

Sarah returned to Edinburgh on June 6th. A date for the administration of the Oath had been set for the 14th. She continued her walks around the city, and the weather continued to alternate between oppressive heat and sharp east winds. By the 10th she complained of being ill again and her mood was not improved by a meeting she had with John Bell and his wife that evening. She had gone round to their house at Bell's invitation. After the two women had eaten together, Bell came home drunk and started to abuse Sarah. He insisted that she was driving Hazlitt to distraction with her demands for money. The divorce after all was her fault because she had failed to give Hazlitt the love he needed.

Bell carried on in this way while he took Sarah home. At this stage he was so drunk that his son came with him in case he needed help. Bell resented this and threatened to beat his son. Then his anger turned to lust. He wanted to take Sarah to her bedroom and stay with her there. She fended him off and he eventually left her, accompanied by his son. After he was gone Sarah broke down. A doctor was called at one o'clock in the morning of June 11th. He applied a fomentation of chamomile to her stomach to help ease her pain and gave her a large dose of laudanum. Her condition was serious enough for him to call twice more that morning.

Sarah began to recover by midday, but Bell had not finished with her. He came round to her room ostensibly to apologise. He blamed his behaviour on his drunkenness. Sarah did not want his company or his apologies. Although

apologetic, Bell was still amorous. He insisted on her for-
giveness and a kiss. She only wanted to shake his hand, but
then agreed to kiss him on condition that he left her.

For Sarah, the days between the 11th and the 14th June
were taken up by further visits from Bell and other friends
of her husband's. Still drowsy from the effects of laudanum, she had another visitor on the 11th. Ritchie came
to reassure her about Hazlitt's willingness to provide the
money they had agreed and to check that she was still willing to go through with the divorce. He advised her to have
as little to do with Bell as possible. But the advice was hard
to take. Bell and his wife had agreed to act as witnesses in
the divorce proceedings.

Hazlitt continued to use intermediaries to reassure
Sarah that he would follow through on the financial agreement they had made. On the 13th Bell came to see her
again, this time to tell her that Hazlitt had set aside a sum
that he would give to her once she had taken the Oath. But
he still felt the need to explain away his drunken attack on
her. This time he chose to blame Hazlitt rather than the
effects of drink. He alleged that Hazlitt had said demean-
ing things about his wife in a conversation with Bell's wife.
He had thought the conversation 'unfit for any modest
woman's ears', but had been aroused by the picture it gave

of Sarah as a woman who might respond tolerantly to Bell's advances.

Sarah continued to be harried by complications and cross purposes. Her lawyer Gray confirmed on the 13th that Sarah was to take the Oath the next day. When she went to tell the Bells this news, Mrs. Bell hesitated. She was now concerned about the damage to her reputation that any association with Hazlitt's divorce might bring, especially if it was reported in the newspapers. She had doubts about her husband's involvement as well, but grudgingly agreed that if her husband had promised to accompany Sarah he must. The behaviour of the Bells at this point typified for Sarah the equivocations and humiliations of the divorce her husband demanded. Her journal entry for the 13th ends with a characteristically reticent indication of her state:

> In the evening walked to the meadows, to prepare for the next day's trial, as I seemed to fear that I should not be able to go through with it, for my illness, though short, was so violent as to pull me down very much.

On June 14th, Sarah took the Oath. Gray asked the

Commissioners to let Sarah do this in a private room, which they agreed to.

Taking the Oath was a matter of routine and ritual. Sarah was required to kneel and swear with her hand on the Bible that she was telling the truth. The Lord Commissioner acted like a priest. He read out the Oath and Sarah, still kneeling, repeated its words after him. She swore to the truth of her accusation that her husband was an adulterer and that there had been no collusion between them. She was required to acknowledge that if she had not spoken truly, she would invoke all the curses of the Bible on her head.

Once Sarah had taken the Oath, both lawyers acting on behalf of the husband and wife urged the Lord Commissioner to act quickly to make the divorce final. They didn't get far. The Lord Commissioner was conscious of the court's reputation. He ruled that the proceedings could not be completed for another five weeks. The witnesses to Hazlitt's adultery would have to be re-examined. Hazlitt's lawyer would need to see the evidence laid against him and decide whether to contest it. Sarah would need to stand before the witness to Hazlitt's contrived adultery at Mrs. Knight's lodging house, so that the witness could confirm that she was not the woman Hazlitt had been seen with. Nothing to do with the divorce was going to happen quickly.

Hazlitt was not in Edinburgh when his wife took the Oath of Calumny. On June 9th he had gone back to Renton Inn, where two months earlier he had written most of the second volume of *Table Talk*. One reason for his stay at Renton was to try and write, but, in the event, all he managed to do was send one letter to Patmore that he had written before his arrival, and write another one. The first letter responded to some questions about Hazlitt's state that Patmore had asked in a letter of his own. Understandably, Patmore thought that Hazlitt's denunciations of Sarah as a whore suggested that what he really wanted was to finish with her. Hazlitt vehemently rejected the suggestion. His love for Sarah was his life's meaning. Without her, he was condemned to an isolated misery:

> Instead of that delicious feeling I had when she was
> heavenly-kind to me and my heart softened and
> melted in its own tenderness and her sweetness,
> I am now inclosed in a dungeon of despair. The sky
> is marble like my thoughts, nature is dead without
> me as hope is within me, no object can give me

one gleam of satisfaction now or the prospect of it
in time to come.

The second letter, written the following day, shows
Hazlitt returning to his obsession with Sarah's sexual
behaviour. In it he reports the conversation he had overheard in the kitchen about penis size. This launches Hazlitt
into an anxious reflection about what Sarah really wants:

> …Can there be a doubt, when the mother dilates on
> cod-pieces and the son replies in measured terms
> that the girl runs mad for size? Miss is small, and
> exaggerates dimensions by contrast. Misjudging fair!
> Yet it is she whom I have spared a hundred times
> from witnessing this consummation devoutly to be
> wished by the whole kitchen in chorus, after she has
> been rubbing against me, hard at it for an hour
> together, thinking to myself, 'The girl is a good girl
> etc. and means no harm – it is only the fondness for
> me, not her lech after a man…'

Hazlitt changes from a tragic into a comic victim of his
passion, a figure whose concern to think well of Sarah –
'The girl is a good girl' – denies him the pleasure he might

have enjoyed and that she seems to want.

His passion might have made Hazlitt comical, but it did not make him less obsessive. As in earlier letters to Patmore, Hazlitt wanted to hit on a plan that would show what Sarah was really like. He invented pretexts for Patmore to visit Sarah: to pick up a manuscript and tell her that Hazlitt had decided to leave Southampton Buildings or, in a ruse that clearly gave Hazlitt some pleasure, to tell her that he would be travelling abroad but wanted to keep his lodgings while he was away. These were intended to provoke a reaction in her, to see how she would respond. If these proved unsuccessful, Hazlitt still had his other plan, that a friend would 'try' Sarah – to find out if she really was willing to have sex with other men, which she either denied to him or that he was too hesitant to take.

Hazlitt found no peace at Renton Inn. By June 15th, he was back in Edinburgh. In his absence the rumour mill had been hard at work. After she had taken the Oath of Calumny, Sarah Hazlitt went to have supper with the Bells. They were clearly eager to tell her the latest news about her husband: that he had gone to Renton Inn; that he had £90 with him that would be used to pay her now she had taken the Oath; that Hazlitt was in a mad state, accusing

Sarah of being a mean cheat and saying that she had no business concerning herself with the welfare of their son. Hazlitt's frenzy was so great that Mrs. Bell told Sarah 'she had been frightened into hysterics'.

Sarah found these stories troubling, but she also doubted their truth. They seemed at odds with her sense of Hazlitt's behaviour towards her and she told the Bells as much. After her supper with them, Sarah went to see Ritchie, hoping for reassurance. He doubted that Hazlitt had as much money as the Bells claimed. Whether he knew about Murray's generosity towards Hazlitt is not clear. If he did, he didn't want Sarah to know about it.

Once Sarah knew that her husband had returned to Edinburgh she tried to arrange a meeting with him. She needed direct assurance about the money he had agreed to give her. The school term was about to end and she was anxious about what arrangements had been made for the care of their son during his holiday. Edinburgh was having its familiar effect on her. She was physically unwell, isolated and continually dependent upon others for money, information and advice: 'I was so nervous and hysterical I could not stay in the house.' She went once more to the Bells' house and insisted that they help her arrange a meeting with Hazlitt. Otherwise she would leave for

London straight away to take care of her son and the divorce proceedings would come to an end.

Sarah did meet Hazlitt, as much by luck as by design. She shuttled between the Bells' house and his lodgings and eventually encountered him, as she recorded in her journal, 'by the way'. Hazlitt gave her some money and reassured her about arrangements for young William's care. Sarah told him that she wanted nothing more to do with the Bells and asked him to use Ritchie as a go-between.

By this stage Hazlitt was becoming anxious that they would be seen talking together. He wanted to bring the conversation to an end, but Sarah was still concerned about money. Hazlitt told her that everything would be settled through Ritchie.

Yet, as Sarah's journal entry makes clear, there was more she wanted to say to her husband. She was disturbed by what the Bells had told her about Hazlitt's behaviour since his return to Edinburgh. According to Mrs. Bell, he had taken to reading his letters to Patmore out loud while walking with her and her husband:

...he pulled [the letter] out of his pocket twenty times, and wanted 'to read' it to them... he talked so loud and acted so extravagantly that the people stood and stared at them as they passed, and seemed to take him for a madman.

It is hard to know how calculated this behaviour was. Since the end of May, and his boat trip back from London to Edinburgh, Hazlitt had been increasingly inclined to display his unhappiness in public. His letters to Patmore and his son – 'Everyone pities poor father, but the monster who has destroyed him' – show how conscious he was of the responses his behaviour might provoke. There is a strong atmosphere of performance in all this, of him *wanting* to be taken for a madman. Certainly, Hazlitt's behaviour on other occasions suggests that he was quite lucid.

The Bells had more gossip to relay to Sarah. In their view Patmore was playing a double game, reassuring Hazlitt that he still had a chance with Sarah Walker while successfully seducing her himself. This time Sarah Hazlitt found their story convincing. Her journal entry for that day, June 17th, ends with a set of statements whose sequence is telling:

Walked to the Glasgow Canal: seemed so restless; as

if I should go mad; and could not swallow I was so choked.

The thought of her husband's public weirdness and private humiliation added to Sarah's distress about what their divorce had inflicted upon her. As their marriage approached its end, its miseries seemed to multiply.

CHAPTER TEN
CONFIDENCES

The Hazlitts' divorce was finalised a month later, on July 17th. In the month before this, Hazlitt stayed in Edinburgh and wrote more letters to Patmore rehearsing his familiar sorrows. He brooded over the significance of the kitchen conversation, and constantly lamented his failure to take Sarah sexually when the opportunity had seemed to be there. He continued to experience the world around him as a living death: 'She was my life – it is gone from me, and I am grown spectral' is how he describes his state in a letter to Patmore of June 20th. He returned to the possibility of 'trying' Sarah, and suggested that Patmore take on the role in a letter begun on July 3rd. But, for all his anger and sorrow, he still refused to give up on the idea that Sarah might marry him once he was divorced. What he needed was someone to support his belief that this still might be possible. In a letter written on June 28th, he asked Patmore if he would visit Sarah's brother-in-law, Robert Roscoe, and ask his advice. By early July, Hazlitt received encouraging news. According to Patmore, Sarah was 'still to be won by wise and prudent conduct on your part'. What Roscoe advised is less clear, but he did not suggest that Hazlitt's plan was hopeless. He also vouched for Sarah's character. Hazlitt's hopes were renewed by these few words from other people.

Sarah Hazlitt came back to Edinburgh on June 28th, and occasionally saw her husband before the divorce was finalised. Both understood that the proceedings were in their final stage. They argued about money. Hazlitt complained about Sarah's travelling expenses, but did tell her about the money that Murray had given him.

Their longest and most intense meeting came after she had been to court on July 17th. In the morning Bell testified that he had known Sarah and Hazlitt as a married couple. Sarah was then presented to Mrs. Knight, who confirmed that Sarah was not the woman Hazlitt had been with at her lodging house on James Street. The Lord Commissioner was satisfied that enough evidence had been presented and agreed to make a legal end to the Hazlitts' marriage.

The first thing Sarah did was seek a meeting with the man who was now her ex-husband. They met that afternoon at Sarah's lodgings and, by her account, their conversation was free of any bitterness or reproach. Hazlitt explained the agitated mood that had led him to criticise her in a conversation with the Bells. She told him about Bell's attempt to seduce her, and what she had heard about Patmore's seduction of Sarah Walker. Hazlitt doubted the story could be true, and went on to tell his wife the history of his love affair with Sarah Walker. Sarah Hazlitt had no difficulty responding to these confidences. She discussed with him his taste in women. Both had recently seen at Dalkeith House 'Hope Finding Fortune in the Sea', a picture that included a female nude. Hazlitt thought it like Sarah Walker. In a letter to Patmore he wrote that the sight of the picture 'drove me mad'. His wife did not agree, as her journal makes clear:

> ...he thought that it was nothing but the winning softness and fondness of her manners which he had never met with in any other women that inveigled him. For she was not at all pretty... and had a poor,

slimy watery look. Yet she was well made and had handsome arms. I said it did not appear to me at all the sort of beauty he used to admire which was plump, and she was as thin & bony as the scrag end of a neck of mutton. That I thought the female figure in the picture at Dalkeith house much more to his taste: he fancied it was like her. I said it was much nearer my form in the thighs, the fall of the back and the contours of the whole figure. He said, I was very well made...

Their divorce may have freed them into this kind of conversation, but it seems to carry in it a history of earlier talks. This may not have been the 'language of love' that Hazlitt wanted, but its openness and frankness makes a vivid contrast with the stifling exchanges he had with Sarah Walker. Hazlitt perhaps had the intimacy he longed for in his marriage. At least he was prepared to accept that his wife was still attractive and Sarah clearly did not think she had lost her husband because she was no longer desirable.

Sarah Hazlitt's directness with her husband seemed to put him at ease. He confessed to her that 'he was only sorry he had not ravished [Sarah Walker] the first week he came into the house'. He explained the misunderstanding with the publishers that had led to the embarrassing appearance of his love affair with Sarah in his essay, *On Great and Little Things*.

He thought that, instead of pursuing Sarah Walker, he should marry a woman of 'good fortune', so 'that he might not be under the necessity of writing another line'. He trusted that his ex-wife would be financially secure and discussed with her arrangements for the care of their son. Their conversation ended in good humour.

If Sarah Hazlitt's journal entry for July 17th showed a camaraderie between an ex-husband and an ex-wife, it also contained some strange revelations about what had been happening in Southampton Buildings. Hazlitt had spoken bluntly about the character of Sarah's mother, Mrs. Walker:

> He said that the mother was the most disgusting, vulgar, old wretch that could be and corrupted her children's minds by her bawdy indecent conversation, though he had never heard an improper or indelicate word from the girl.

This repeats what Hazlitt had already written to Patmore. He had heard nothing 'improper or indelicate' from Sarah. But something altogether stranger pointed in another direction:

> ...it had often struck him, that they never objected to the girls of the town coming up to him continually, and that Sarah would often send them up when his mother said he was not at home...

Sarah was content to usher prostitutes into Hazlitt's room, even if this went against her mother's wishes. As far as Sarah Hazlitt was concerned, this confirmed her view that Southampton Buildings was not a respectable lodging house, and may have acted like a brothel. In their conversation neither she nor Hazlitt speculated about the effects these visits might have had on Sarah Walker. But it helps us understand one of the many motives Sarah might have had for refusing to have sex with a man who was convinced he needed to marry her.

The day before this conversation, Hazlitt had started a letter to Patmore, who was about to get married and travel with his wife in Europe. The contrast provoked some familiar brooding in Hazlitt about his own unhappiness. He was still drawn to the melodramatic grandeur of seeing himself as an outcast: '...on my forehead alone is written – REJECTED'. But he continued to work on the idea of his future happiness with Sarah, this time adding a new twist to how it might be achieved:

> If she will but have me, I'll make her love me: and I think her not giving a positive answer looks like it, and also shews that there is no one else. Her holding out to the last also, I think, proves that she was never to be gained but with honour. She's a strange inscrutable girl: but if I once win her consent I shall kill her with kindness.

This time the plan was to get Sarah to agree to marry him, regardless of her feelings for him. Once she had adopted the role of wife, the strength of his love for her would elicit a corresponding feeling in her. The very thing that he had told himself and his son was impossible a few months earlier he was now prepared to believe.

Hazlitt completed his letter to Patmore with a single sentence, added the day after the divorce was completed: 'It is all over, & I am my own man, and yours ever.' After some confusion about whether to leave by mail-coach or boat, Hazlitt left for London by sea on the morning of July 18th. Sarah Hazlitt stayed on in Edinburgh a little longer.

She took shelter that evening from a heavy thunderstorm in one of Edinburgh's new attractions, a panorama of the bay of Naples. Hazlitt, meanwhile, had convinced himself once again that the 'road to paradise' was still open.

CHAPTER ELEVEN
THE END OF THE AFFAIR

Hazlitt arrived back in London on either the 20th or 21st July. He immediately went to Southampton Buildings to meet Sarah. The most detailed account of what happened between them is Hazlitt's own. It takes the form of a letter ostensibly written to James Sheridan Knowles in the late summer of 1822. But it is highly unlikely that the letter was ever sent, or that Hazlitt ever intended it to be. What he was doing instead was using letters as a literary form in his *Liber Amoris*, which he had been working on since the beginning of 1822. It reminds us that, while Hazlitt may have been captivated by Sarah Walker, he was also intent on turning his passion into print.

Patmore and Roscoe, Sarah's brother-in-law, had strengthened his belief that Sarah might still agree to marry him. Crucially, this meeting would be different from all the others because he was now free to make a serious proposal of marriage to her. Their first encounter in his sitting room proved ambiguous. Sarah was polite but distant. The mood was not as explosive as it had been when they had seen each other in May. Hazlitt tried to interpret her reticence as a sign in his favour:

> She still absented herself from the room, but was mild and affable when she did come. She was pale, dejected, evidently uneasy about something and had plainly been ill. I thought it was perhaps her reluctance to yield to my wishes, her pity for what I suffered; and that in the struggle between both she did not know what to do. How I worshipped her at these moments!

Hazlitt wanted to persuade himself that he was on Sarah's mind in a way that was not simply oppressive to her. He wanted to recreate, or at least recall, their intimacy. Small acts might help to do this. A few days after his arrival, she agreed to put new frills on his shirts. She also arranged to have the 'little image' mended – the statue of Napoleon that Hazlitt had broken in his rage at her rejection of him in May. He tried to persuade her to make some silk he had given her into a summer gown.

These nervous, delicate exchanges encouraged Hazlitt. He talked to Sarah about one of their possible futures together: that they might be special friends. Sarah began to cry and this provoked a strange kind of rapture in Hazlitt:

> ...so she stood... with the tears trickling from her eye-lashes, her head stooping, her attitude fixed, with the finest expression that ever was seen of mixed regret, pity, and stubborn resolution; but without speaking a word, without altering a feature. It was like a petrification of a human face in the softest moment of passion.

Whether this is an accurate account of Hazlitt's experience at the time or an elaboration of it after the event is impossible to tell. Certainly passages like this raise again the question of Hazlitt's invention of his love affair with Sarah. Either way, the scene is familiar. Hazlitt talks and Sarah doesn't. But whether at the time or in hindsight, the scene took on a deeper significance. Sarah became expressive without the need for words. He was like a witness to a wonderful work of art. Weeping Sarah, 'like a petrification of a human face in the softest moment of passion', became an example of something Hazlitt valued highly. In an essay written in 1816, Hazlitt had given a name to this value. He called it 'gusto'.

'Gusto' — literally the Italian word for taste — identified a quality of intense expression that Hazlitt found in the paintings of Titian, Michelangelo and Caravaggio. But it didn't only apply to the visual arts. He found the same quality in Milton's poetry, in Boccaccio and Rabelais, and in John Gay's *Beggars Opera*. Pictures came to life through 'gusto' and so did dramatic characters on a stage, or lines of poetry, or stories in a book. For Hazlitt, 'gusto' came to point to all experiences of intense and heightened sensation. They stood out from the ordinary course of life and, although they were often found in art and literature, these experiences could be discovered anywhere:

There is hardly any object entirely devoid of expression; without some character of power belonging to it, some precise association with pleasure or pain...

His love affair with Sarah Walker in a lodging house in

Holborn was no exception. An eerie sense of fulfilment hovers around his description of her, 'with tears trickling from her eyelashes', as though he had encountered the highest degree of 'gusto' that she was capable of in her relation to him. Her silence is transfigured into 'the finest expression that ever was seen'. His repeated comparison of Sarah with a statue now evokes 'the softest moment of passion', not a cold rejection of Hazlitt's efforts to love her.

All the requirements of courtship, all the manoeuverings that might lead to marriage, fell away for a moment. Hazlitt could contemplate Sarah as he might a work of art, and be moved by her. These intensities could as well be savoured at the end of an affair as at its beginning. They didn't have to fit into a story with a happy or an unhappy ending. But, in practice, Hazlitt could not of course be content with contemplation alone. He couldn't make that the point of his affair with Sarah. He still wanted to marry her and that meant he wanted to find out what was making her cry. And, as before, his pursuit of explanations drove her away. She refused to answer his questions and left his sitting room.

The pattern of their behaviour together seemed to have established itself with a machine-like regularity: fragile agreements, brief moments of happiness, followed by separation once Hazlitt tried to make their relationship into something that Sarah did not want it to be. One thing that Hazlitt had learnt was to control his misery and anger when Sarah rejected him. He was intent now on playing a waiting game and looking out for encouraging signs. He stayed on in Southampton Buildings, encouraged by Sarah's willingness to do the things he asked – the frills on his shirt, the repair of the little statue.

These signs of hope did not stop Sarah from keeping out of his way. He wanted to talk, but she didn't. Despite his deep unease about the role she played in Sarah's life, Hazlitt turned to Sarah's mother for advice. Mrs. Walker told him that Sarah had been too busy with arrangements for repairing the statue to have time to see him. His worries were exaggerated. Sarah was what he wanted her to be: dutiful, affectionate, giving priority to his concerns.

Again Hazlitt's mood was changed by some encouraging words. He now proposed to transform Southampton Buildings in a way that would make his presence there acceptable to Sarah. He agreed with Mrs. Walker that he would rent most of the rooms in the lodging house for 100 guineas a year. Sarah would be released from any further need to work and this would improve her health. But

Hazlitt's fantasy went beyond this. He imagined a masochist's contract with Sarah. She would be the mistress of the house and he would become her slave:

> ...I took nearly the whole of the lodgings at a hundred guineas a year, that (as I said) she might have a little leisure to sit at her needle of an evening... She was not in good health, and it would do her good to be less confined. I would be the drudge and she should no longer be the slave. I asked nothing in return. To see her happy, to make her so, was to be so myself...

This, in Hazlitt's mind, was the offer that Sarah could not refuse. He was so delighted with the idea that he decided to take an evening walk down to Blackheath so that he could continue to dream about his future happiness. He needed to persuade himself that what he wanted to happen had already happened. He seemed oblivious to the fact that the arrangement had been made in Sarah's absence without her agreement.

Hazlitt stayed the night at Blackheath and, according to his own account, spent 'the whole of the next morning on the heath under the open sky, dreaming of my earthly

Goddess'. By the evening he was back at Southampton Buildings. His dream of happiness continued. Sarah came to his room and gave him the statue of Napoleon, repaired. They held hands. Hazlitt begged her to say yes to his offer of marriage. She said nothing, but, as at their first meeting, she looked into his eyes. Hazlitt wanted to believe, as before, that her gaze was the true indication of her feelings, and that those feelings were of compassionate love towards him.

The next morning, Monday July 29th, Hazlitt sat in his room and made marriage plans. He would take Sarah and her mother to Scotland by Wednesday. By Saturday he and Sarah would be married at Gretna Green. He hesitated to go downstairs and make his proposal. 'Something', as he put it in his letter to Knowles, 'withheld me.' Whatever that something was – perhaps a sense of the futility of his plans – his need to see Sarah increased. Again he found a pretext in the statue for a meeting. He needed to pay her for its repair. He went downstairs and asked Sarah's younger sister, Betsey, to pass the message on. She told him that Sarah had gone out to visit her grandmother who lived nearby in Somers Town. This news made Hazlitt anxious. It reminded him of something he had noticed since his return. Sarah had seemed to be going out more often than she had when he first knew her. When at home he had also noticed that she was in a state of expectation, 'sitting in the window seat of the front parlour' and looking out into the street. Something was drawing her away from the place that had defined her life.

Hazlitt left the house to track her down. He walked northwards towards Somers Town, anticipating that he would meet Sarah on her way back from her grandmother's. He had not been walking long when he saw her face emerge out of the city crowd coming towards him. He at first thought she was on her own, but then realised that Sarah was walking with a 'tall, rather well-looking young man'.

What followed was a strange kind of dance. Hazlitt, Sarah and her companion walked past each other without acknowledgement. They stopped, turned, looked at each other, and then walked on. Nothing was said.

Hazlitt returned to his lodging house but could not stay there. He went back into the street and met the couple again coming towards Southampton Buildings. When Sarah entered the lodging house alone, Hazlitt followed her and immediately asked her to talk to him. He knew what she feared – another outburst of his hysterical rage – and was determined to keep his composure.

Their conversation, according to Hazlitt, was marked by a deliberate and carefully managed courtesy. Sarah confirmed what Hazlitt suspected. The 'rather well-looking young man' was John Tomkins, the lawyer who had lodged in Southampton Buildings between the autumn of 1821 and the spring of 1822. Sarah suggested that there was little significance in their walking together. Hazlitt expressed his concern for Sarah's reputation. Sarah insisted that there was nothing threatening in what she was doing. Hazlitt discovered that Tomkins had left the lodging house because he had wanted to cool his relationship with Sarah but that the couple continued to meet out of doors. Hazlitt maintained his concerned tone. Assuming that she had been as intimate with Tomkins as she had been with him, he was worried that Tomkins might gain control over her. This did not go down well. Sarah briefly thanked Hazlitt for his advice and made to leave the room. He, thinking this might be the last time they talked together, asked for a kiss. Sarah refused him and left.

Hazlitt 'felt deep grief', but was determined to be stoic in his defeat. He had lost out to a rival. There was very little he could do about that. In the face of this disappointment he couldn't tolerate his room so, once again, he went out, hoping, perhaps, to walk off the effects of the initial shock or to find somebody to share his sorrow. He hadn't been walking long when he met Tomkins.

What happened next was deeply characteristic. Instead of avoiding Tomkins, Hazlitt asked if they could talk. Candour, even in the most difficult circumstances, was an important value for Hazlitt. He wanted to hear what his successful rival had to say and find out his version of events.

The two men talked for four hours. Their conversation confirmed Hazlitt's earlier suspicions about Sarah's behaviour. While the two men were lodgers at Southampton Buildings, Sarah had become intimate with both of them. She had developed a routine, bringing Tomkins his breakfast and spending an hour with him and then, later in the day, moving on to Hazlitt to do the same thing. To each she denied her affection for the other. The story of her former lover was used to divert Hazlitt's attentions away from her romance with Tomkins. While the outcome of that relationship remained uncertain, she had maintained an ambivalent stance towards Hazlitt. When things with Tomkins looked promising she rejected Hazlitt; when they went less well she became more affectionate.

This was the version of events that the two men agreed on. However disappointed he may have felt, Hazlitt also experienced a kind of relief. His uncertainty was over and it was some consolation to him that Sarah's lover was Tomkins – a rival in love he respected – and not the virile apothecary, Griffiths, who had provoked his most jealous fantasies. Still, his letter to Knowles shows his propensity to project his sufferings on a grand scale. Sarah's rejection was an apocalyptic event, destroying the possibility of any more of the emotional intensities of the previous months:

I am no more lifted now to Heaven, and then plunged in the abyss; but I seem to have been thrown from the top of a precipice, and to be grov-elling, stunned, and stupefied. I am melancholy, lonesome, and weaker than a child.

CHAPTER TWELVE
LOVE AT LAST SIGHT

Hazlitt was like Milton's Satan, suffering the consequences of a great fall, but lacking Satan's rebellious
spirit. At least the giddying movement, the intense oscilla-
tion between hope and despair, was over. He was no longer
torn between two incompatible images of Sarah. Rather,
he became fascinated by their interaction.

Sarah had become to him a special kind of heroine.
Despite his past tendency to think of her in terms of
precedents drawn from literature and painting he now
regarded her as something new: 'a more complete experiment in character was never made'. For Hazlitt, Sarah
stepped outside the traditional classifications of women
as either Madonna or whore. She sustained a novel and

powerful kind of hypocrisy:

> ...it is one faultless, undeviating, consistent, con-
> summate piece of acting. Were she a saint on earth
> she could not seem more like one. Her hypocritical
> high flown pretensions, indeed, make her the worse:
> but still the ascendancy of her will, her determined
> perseverance in what she undertakes to do, has
> something admirable in it, approaching to the
> heroic.

What he found in her was a capacity for self-invention
that was more than a match for his own. It was as though
he couldn't stop himself from being the theatre critic, full
of admiration for her stunning performance.

Hazlitt was left with the ruins of his passion. After a
sleepless night he came to the dawn-light conviction that
his love for Sarah was an illusion. He still felt the pulse
of what he described as a 'fatal passion', but that was now
something distinct in his mind from love. The separation
from Sarah was final. The question for him became what
to do with the illusion he had created around her. In the
letter to Knowles he presents a mixture of horror, mourn-
ing and pathos:

I had embraced the false Florimel instead of the true, and was like the man in the Arabian nights who had married a ghoul.

Hazlitt's imagination worked upon the nature of his loss, finding analogies, precedents and quotations that provided him with some consolation and a kind of understanding. Evoking literary precedents reminded him that he was not the first to suffer in this way. It also reminded him that his loss had been the source of stories and affecting images. But imagination also became the way to turn the end of his affair into a means of prolonging his love. Sarah might be lost to him as a lover or a wife but she was perpetually alive in his recollection of 'what she once was to me'. Hazlitt decided to cherish his illusion. He would – like his contemporary, the poet Coleridge – be constant to an ideal of love that he had experienced.

At the end of the letter to Knowles, Hazlitt thinks of his cherished image of Sarah receding from him over time, 'like a weed that the wave bears farther and farther from me'. So he keeps sight of her as she moves further away; his helpless contemplation acts as an anaesthetic against the pain of loss. He anticipates that at some point her image will be lost to him for ever, but not yet. Hazlitt wanted some time to become bored with Sarah. Even in his imagination she would lose her special status.

The letter to Knowles is suffused with a bittersweet sense of an ending. The reality in Southampton Buildings was a little different. Despite what had happened to him, Hazlitt stayed on there. On August 24th, nearly a month after Sarah's final rejection of him, he wrote from there to Francis Jeffrey to discuss work for the *Edinburgh Review*. He gave a terse account of what had happened – 'I have since I returned found out the person I told you of to be a regular lodging-house decoy'– and apologised to Jeffrey for his distracted state during his stay in Edinburgh. He described himself as 'better a good deal', but this improvement was not always obvious to others. Two weeks before he wrote to Jeffrey, Hazlitt had visited the painter Benjamin Robert Haydon, at his house in Lisson Grove. Haydon gave a brief record of Hazlitt's visit in his diary entry for August 9th:

Hazlitt called last night in a state of absolute insanity about the girl who has jilted him. Poor Hazlitt, his candour is great and his unaffected frankness is interesting.

This was not the first time that Hazlitt had called on Haydon to talk about his rejection. Earlier in the month he had talked to him in a way that had filled Haydon with disgust. Hazlitt had gone into too much sordid detail for Haydon's pious ears, as another journal entry records:

Down he goes, sleeps in a brothel with a strumpet, one-eyed from disease, his wife brings her action & he is divorced. By heavens! There is something so disgusting in this it makes the gorge rise.

For Haydon the story that Hazlitt felt compelled to tell provoked different reactions: disgust at its impropriety, a diagnosis of madness, and a more sympathetic understanding of Hazlitt's 'unaffected frankness'. Like Rousseau, Hazlitt did not want a society based upon secrecy. His own behaviour has a sense of revolutionary demonstration about it. A society of equals would be a society of frankness. He would say what he thought even if other people wanted him to be discreet.

Another record of his need to talk about his passion indicates how rapidly he could perceive his own behaviour ironically. The writer Barry Procter (who also wrote under the pseudonym Barry Cornwall) met Hazlitt shortly after his rejection by Sarah. He thought Hazlitt the victim of 'an insane passion'. But the echo of Hazlitt's speaking voice that we get from Procter's account of their meeting suggests that this is not the whole story:

'I am a cursed fool' said he to me. 'I saw J— going into Will's Coffee-house yesterday morning; he spoke to me. I followed him into the house; and whilst he lunched I told him the whole story.' 'Then' (said he) 'I wandered into Regent's Park, where I met one of M—'s sons. I walked with him some time, and on his using some civil expression, by God! Sir, I told him the whole story.' ... 'Well sir' (he went on) 'I then went to Haydon; but he was out. There was only his man, Salmon, there: but, by God! I could not help myself. It all came out: the whole cursed story! Afterwards I went to look at some lodgings in Pimlico. The landlady at one place, after some explanations as to rent, etc. said to me very kindly, "I'm afraid you are not well, sir?" – "No, ma'am," said I, "I am not well;" and on inquiring further, the devil take me if I did not let out the whole story, from beginning to end!'

Hazlitt may have been in the grip of an obsession, going out on the town to find a sympathetic ear whenever the opportunity arose. But he also could see the comedy in his repetitive behaviour. He was gripped by the story he had to tell, but was not deluded about what he was doing.

Hazlitt was not the only person talking about his love affair, nor were Haydon and Cornwall the only people noting the oddity of his behaviour. In August the reviews of the second volume of *Table Talk* came through. The Tory press took this as an opportunity to renew their attacks on him. Some of these repeated familiar themes: Hazlitt was an egotistical writer; his style was exhibitionistic and confusing. But a sentence in a hostile review published in the *Monthly Literary Register* for August 2nd sounded a new note: 'let us have no more of his landlord's daughter in italics...'

The second volume of *Table Talk* contained essays such as *On Great and Little Things* and *On the Knowledge of Character* where Hazlitt declared his passion. But, in all of them, Sarah appeared under a pseudonym. We know from his wife's conversation with him that the publication of *On Great and Little Things* earlier in the year had drawn his enemies' attention to the real identity of 'Infelice'. By August hostile journalists were prepared to use their knowledge of

Sarah's identity to attack him in print. As far as the *Monthly Literary Register* was concerned, Sarah's reality was defined by her social status: a 'landlord's daughter'. To see her as the epitome of female beauty and grace was ludicrous and potentially subversive. Beauty was the property of ladies, not of landlords' daughters.

Gossip about Hazlitt's love life had been circulating by word of mouth. Now it was getting into print. At the moment when Hazlitt's hopes for a marriage with Sarah had come to an end, his love life was taking on a new and potentially scandalous existence in newspapers and reviews. Despite his sensitivity to public attacks on his writing and his character, Hazlitt did not respond immediately to the reference to Sarah in the *Monthly Literary Register*. He continued to haunt the scene of his rejection, staying on at Southampton Buildings until the end of August and possibly into September. If he talked to Sarah during this time there is no mention of it in his correspondence or in the diaries kept by his acquaintances.

Haydon's fascination with Hazlitt's state continued, and Hazlitt continued to visit him. A letter Haydon wrote to the writer Mary Mitford bristles with condescension and gossipy excitement. Haydon repeats to her his belief that Hazlitt is insane. But two new things emerge. One is a vivid, if mocking, portrait of Hazlitt's appearance at the time. According to Haydon, Hazlitt talked about love like a young man, but his face was 'old, hard, weather-beaten, saturnine, metaphysical...' Hazlitt's clothes made him seem even more grotesque. He had taken to dressing in the latest style: 'Since this affair he has taken to dressing in the fashion and keeps insinuating his improved appearance. He springs up to show you his pantaloons! What a being it is!' These efforts to appear younger than he was had clearly not impressed Sarah. Hazlitt had the clownish vulnerability of a middle-aged man who had fallen for a much younger woman.

Haydon's letter also had news about the *Liber Amoris*:

He has written down all the conversations without colour, literal as they happened; he has preserved all the love letters, many of which are equal to anything of the sort and really affecting: and I believe, in order to ease his soul of the burden, means with certain arrangements, to publish it as a tale of character. He will sink into idiotcy (sic) if he does not get rid of it...

Hazlitt's plans for the book had changed since he

first wrote to Patmore about it in March. The 'book of our conversations' had grown to include 'love letters', and it was a book that, by September, Hazlitt was planning to publish.

As far as Haydon was concerned, its purpose was clear. It was to act as a cure for Hazlitt's lovesickness. It was also, in Haydon's view, to be a book without artifice, a documentary record of a love affair. Hazlitt was the secretary and clerk of his passion, providing faithful records of conversations and preserving love letters. As a 'tale of character', its emphasis would be on psychology rather than action.

Whether Haydon saw any of the 'love letters' is not clear. He seemed unaware of the fact that some of them were 'unsent', composed specifically for inclusion in the *Liber Amoris*. And most of the letters in the book were not love letters in a conventional sense, but letters about love, based mostly on Hazlitt's correspondence with Patmore. Even before its publication the *Liber Amoris* was liable to be misunderstood, perhaps because of Hazlitt's own excitable talk about it.

By October, Hazlitt had moved from Southampton Buildings to new lodgings at 4 Chapel Street West, just off Curzon Street in Mayfair. The routines of his working life began to reassert themselves. He wrote once again to Francis Jeffrey in early October, proposing some further work for the *Edinburgh Review*. He still felt a need to apologise to Jeffrey for his behaviour in Edinburgh during his divorce. He had kept away from friends and acquaintances there because 'I hated the sight of myself, and fancied that everybody else did the same'. His passion filled him with self-loathing, and he imagined that others loathed him in the same way. He seemed to be aware of his own folly while still feeling compelled to act it out.

Jeffrey responded positively to Hazlitt's proposals for work. Hazlitt consequently began a lengthy essay on the current state of journalism for the *Edinburgh Review*. At the same time he agreed with the editors of the *London Magazine* to write a series of pieces on the picture galleries of England. He began work on this series during a brief visit to Winterslow in late October. By the time he returned to London in November, he had another idea for a book, a collection of aphorisms and reflections that was published the following year with the title *Characteristics*.

In the same month he was invited by Leigh Hunt to contribute to a new journal, the *Liberal*. Hunt had left England for Italy in the spring of 1822 and his conversations there with Shelley and Byron had laid the groundwork for the new publication. Its title declared its political intent. The *Liberal* was to be a journal critical of established power. Its subtitle, *Verse and Prose from the South*, declared its exile status. Shelley's death on July 8th, 1822 had already given the new magazine a posthumous feel. If *The Liberal* was dedicated to the renewal of radicalism, its publication was overshadowed by the death of one of its champions. Leigh Hunt wanted Hazlitt to join him and Byron in Pisa, but by the end of 1822 that was a journey too far for Hazlitt. What he did do was start work on the first of his contributions, an essay called *On the Spirit of Monarchy*, which was published in the first issue of the magazine in January 1823.

His grief and anger over Sarah had not stopped Hazlitt writing for long – at most for a few weeks in the summer of 1822. If contemporary witness is anything to go by, he seemed to be talking less about the affair as the year came to an end. None of this meant that he had worked himself free from his passion and its consequences. Sarah was still present in his imagination, a dark familiar that would not let him go. He continued to work on *Liber Amoris*, passing on a manuscript of the book to Patmore who made a fair copy that Hazlitt corrected. He was still drawn to

Southampton Buildings. He spent evenings watching the lodging house from the street outside, longing to know about Sarah, if only through a brief glimpse of her.

His writing during this period continued to bear the imprint of his experience with Sarah, even when it was about subjects apparently far removed from love. *On the Spirit of Monarchy* is a powerful republican argument against monarchy. Why, he asked, do we admire monarchs even when it is clear that they have no exceptional talents? His answer drew him back to a word that he had used about Sarah:

> ... All we want is to aggrandise our own vain-glory at second hand; and the less of real superiority or excellence there is in the person we fix upon as our proxy in this dramatic exhibition, the more easily can we change places with him... An idol is not the worse for being of coarse materials; a king should be a common-place man... Man is a poetical animal and delights in fiction...We make kings of men, and Gods of stocks and stones: we are not jealous of the creatures of our own hands.

Sarah had been his 'little idol – the dear image in my

heart' in the letter he had written to her in March 1822. He had imagined that the statue of Napoleon – 'that little image' – might play a similar role for Sarah because it reminded her of her former lover. *On the Spirit of Monarchy* reviewed this human tendency to idolatry in much less tender terms. Our admiration of monarchs, according to Hazlitt, is just a kind of narcissism. We can imagine ourselves as them, at the centre of attention, and the more ordinary they are the easier this is to do. He had not quite diagnosed his love for Sarah in these terms, but the conclusion of his fictional letter to Knowles showed him reflecting on the possibility that his love for Sarah had been a case of creating a divine creature out of an ordinary girl.

One of his greatest essays, written in February 1823, and published in the April issue of the *Liberal,* was suffused with a sense of loss. *My First Acquaintance with Poets* recalls a time of hope when Hazlitt first met Coleridge and Wordsworth in 1798. The impact of their personalities and their poetry on the young Hazlitt is remembered as one expression of a time of revolutionary hope. Human nature, it seemed, might change:

Somehow that period (the time just after the French Revolution) was not a time when nothing was given for nothing. The mind opened, and a softness might be perceived coming over the hearts of individuals beneath 'the scales that fence' our self interest.

But the mutuality of that time 'just after the French Revolution', recalled by Hazlitt as a period of vivid communication and expression, had not survived. A part of Hazlitt's disappointment was with the direction his own life had taken since his first meeting with Wordsworth and Coleridge. He looks back upon an existence that had somehow failed to happen:

So have I loitered my life away, reading books, looking at pictures, going to plays, hearing, thinking, writing on what pleases me best. I have wanted only one thing to make me happy, but wanting that have wanted everything.

Hazlitt's regular readers would have recognised that that 'one thing' was the love that he thought had been denied him. There is a mute appeal in Hazlitt's announcement that love has passed him by, as though he might still find someone to supply the 'one thing' that he wants. But a harsher understanding is also at work. The contrast between 1823 and 1798 is heightened by Hazlitt's experience of rejection. No softness had come over Sarah's heart. Their relationship might be an example of that kind of sterile exchange where 'nothing is given for nothing'.

There were also some scores to settle. At times it seemed as if he was defying his enemies to do their worst. In the essay *On the Scotch Character* he described the group of writers who worked for *Blackwood's Magazine* as 'a troop of Yahoos'. The last third of his essay *On the Periodical Press* was devoted to an attack on the 'savage system of bullying and assassination' that he found in Tory newspapers and journals.

Hazlitt felt that these attacks had caused the death of Keats, 'mangled and torn to pieces with ruthless, unfeeling rage'. He had suffered damage as well. But he kept any personal pathos out of the essay. The tone is one of measured defiance. Hazlitt concluded with an argument about the self-defeating nature of the kind of abuse he had suffered:

> ...the extent and extravagance of the abuse has already had the effect, not only of making individual attacks less painful and alarming, but even, in many cases, of pointing out to the judicious the proper

objects of their gratitude and respect. For ourselves, at least, we do not hesitate to acknowledge that, when we find an author savagely and perseveringly attacked by this gang of literary retainers, we feel assured, not only that he is a good writer, but an honest man.

In the early months of 1823 Hazlitt may have been squaring up for another round with his political and literary enemies, knowing that they had information about his pursuit of Sarah Walker that they could use against him. Her rejection of him continued to impress itself on his work like a watermark.

Other consequences of his passion, some financial, some emotional, continued to affect his life. In February he was arrested for debt, the result of unpaid costs from his divorce. He wrote for help to his young friend and admirer, Thomas Noon Talfourd who promptly secured his release.

His old obsession with testing Sarah still flared up in him. He wanted to know whether she was a modest girl or a 'boarding house jilt'. This produced the last and possibly the most perverse incident in the story of his passion.

In early March, Hazlitt persuaded a friend of his to

masquerade as a lodger at 9 Southampton Buildings. Who this friend was is not certain; in the journal Hazlitt kept, recording the results of this experiment, he was simply identified as Mr. F. It may have been the strangely named Albany Fonblanque, an assistant to Hazlitt's friend, John Black. Though Mr. F.'s identity is uncertain, what he had to do was not. He had first to flirt with Sarah and then persuade her to have sex with him. Mr. F. agreed terms for renting a room from Mrs. Walker on March 4th and moved into Southampton Buildings on the following day. His testing of Sarah was to last for the next eleven days.

Hazlitt's journal for this period provides a troubled account of what took place. It was first published in 1900 by Hazlitt's great nephew, William Carew Hazlitt. He misleadingly presented it as part of the *Liber Amoris* and thought it referred to events in 1822. A further version of the journal was published in 1959, although it was not until 1971 that a reliable text became available.

In the end the experiment didn't reveal anything that Hazlitt didn't already know. Sarah flirted with Mr. F. By March the 8th he had 'kissed her several times on the stair case, at which she laughed'. She brought Mr. F. his breakfast, talked to him in his room and let him kiss her. Physical contact became more intimate. Hazlitt detailed each move in the game: 'his hand upon her thigh, to which she made not the slightest objection'; and then, in a meeting in the corridor, 'F. got her between his legs so that she came in complete contact with him.' Then he went too far:

Saturday March 15th. She did not come up in the morning and nothing was done (she was altered in her manner and began to smoke [suspect] something)... but as she put down the curtains at night, he kissed her and saying he was determined to give her a good tickling for her tricks in running away from him the day before, put his hand between her legs without ceremony. She only said 'Let me go Sir', and returning to the door, asked if he would have the fire lighted. She did not come up again.

Hazlitt's journal for this period is a disturbed and disturbing document. If his experiment on Sarah proved nothing, it none the less allowed Hazlitt to revisit the scene of his loss and the emotions it provoked in him. Different people play out the same roles. Tomkins is mentioned. Sarah was 'seen in close conference with him' by Mr. F., and this news provoked Hazlitt's envy. Tomkins seemed to possess a verbal magic that Hazlitt didn't have. He wondered 'what divine music he poured into her ear, to which my words were harsh discord'. But as Mr. F.'s attempted seduction of Sarah continued, Hazlitt developed an uneasy sympathy for Tomkins. He was now occupying the position that Hazlitt had once occupied, the betrayed lover. Sarah became a flirtatious goddess, moving around the lodging house and deciding men's fates.

Hazlitt used F.'s reports to bolster his contempt for Sarah. She was a 'little ideot'; she pretended to a morality that she didn't practise; and she lacked taste. F.'s attempt to seduce her was accompanied by questions assessing the depth of her reading in contemporary literature in an effort to prove that she had no literary judgement.

Throughout his journal Hazlitt intoned with increasing sarcasm the advice that Sarah's aunt had given her, and that she had relayed to him. She must be 'determined to keep every lodger at a proper distance'. He needed to exorcise his passion by convincing himself that Sarah was worthless. But no amount of invective against her could conceal the fact that she had rejected him and that he still longed to be intimate with her. Some passages in his journal can begin in fury and end in wistful longing:

Decoy! Damned, treble damned ideot! When shall I

burn her out of my thoughts? Yet I like to hear about her. That she had her bed gown or her ruff on, is to me a visitation from heaven – to know that she is a whore or an idiot is better than nothing. Were I in Hell, my only consolation would be to learn of her. In Heaven to see her would be my only reward.

F.'s testing of Sarah was a perverse and forlorn expression of Hazlitt's need to get close to her. If he could no longer be in Southampton Buildings, it was better than nothing to have someone there who could report on her. Knowing anything, however bad, was better than knowing nothing.

Meanwhile, Hazlitt was completing a different literary experiment. On May 9th John Hunt, Leigh Hunt's brother and a champion of press freedom, published *Liber Amoris*. He paid Hazlitt £100 for the copyright. The book was published anonymously in contrast to the two volumes of *Table Talk*. The brief advertisement or introduction that followed the book's title page stated that its author had died of 'disappointment preying on a sickly frame and morbid state of mind'.

The fiction about the book's origins and authorship may have been an attempt on Hazlitt's part to cover his tracks.

What is equally likely is that he was announcing what kind of a book the *Liber Amoris* was. Like *La Nouvelle Heloise* and *The Sorrows of Young Werther* before it, *Liber Amoris* was a story of a 'fatal attachment'. The advertisement states that the book's publication was the fulfilment of an obligation to the dead. Its author saw the work as a memento of 'his strongest feeling while living'.

As Haydon had indicated in his letter to Mary Mitford, *Liber Amoris* had changed since Hazlitt first conceived the book at the beginning of 1822. 'The book of our conversations', with the addition of two edited versions of letters Hazlitt had sent to Sarah, had become the first of three parts. The second part consisted of edited letters Hazlitt had written to Patmore during the spring and summer of 1822 and included one letter from Patmore, identified as C.P. in the text. The third part was made up of the fictional letter Hazlitt had written to J.S.K., a surrogate for his Glasgow friend, James Sheridan Knowles. Other brief texts are interspersed throughout the book: lines 'written in a blank leaf' of Keats's poem, *Endymion*, a story of doomed love; a brief quotation from another unhappy love story, Shakespeare's *Troilus and Cressida*, under the heading 'A Proposal of Love'. In addition there are brief essays on the nature of love and a melancholy address to Edinburgh:

'Thy cold grey walls reflect back the leaden melancholy of my soul.' The characters' names are given in the form of initials. Hazlitt becomes 'H.' and Sarah 'S.'.

Taken as a whole, the book is like an album or a reliquary of a love affair. This quality is reinforced by aspects of the book's design. Very rarely for a book published by a contemporary writer in this period, the book's title-page includes the cameo-like portrait of the young woman with her eyes upturned that is alluded to by H. in his first conversation with S. The renaissance style of the portrait hints at a kind of beauty that may be found only in the past, just as the book's title and sub-title suggest a question about the survival of a past language and mythology into modern times.

Liber Amoris may be the history of a powerful passion, and it may, in large part, be written in the form of confessional letters. But none of this stops it from being an artful book. Hazlitt treated his original letters to Patmore like a first draft. Sentences from one letter were moved to another. He included in one of them a passage he had deleted from his essay, *The Fight*. He added passages depicting the different moods of love: the torment of waiting on the beloved's reply, sudden bursts of hope followed by despair, and lonely wanderings in picturesque landscapes. Other passages were omitted, notably the obscene puns, the overheard conversation about Mr. Griffiths' penis, and nearly every mention of publishers, money and the business of making books. This tends to make the book more about love's sensitivities and less about lust. H. is an invention. He is the melancholy victim of a hopeless passion. But not entirely: there are libertine echoes in the book as well. Letter 9 of *Liber Amoris*, based upon a letter sent to Patmore in July 1822, shows H. reflecting on his failure to test S. sexually, and in the same letter he presents her as someone who may be playing the field for her own pleasure. H. shows traces of his notorious fictional predecessor, the libertine Lovelace in Richardson's *Clarissa*. But the libertine sensibility evident in the original letter is comparatively subdued in *Liber Amoris*. H. is a sad hero of love, torn between a belief in the immortality of his love, despite its rejection and his knowledge that love, his own included, like all things, fades.

The artfulness of *Liber Amoris* frames its confessional moments, inviting its readers not just to sympathise with the feelings it portrays but also to analyse them. The absence of names has a role to play here. It's not just the author who is anonymous, his name absent from the title page. The story's characters have a curious anonymity too.

We know them by their initials: H., S., C.P., J.S.K.
Nobody has a name, and nobody calls each other by name.
It is as though they are in transit from being the real characters in a love affair – Hazlitt, Sarah, Patmore – to
becoming abstract roles in a drama about love.

Few books are more telling about the nature of a dis-
tinctively modern solitude, a craving for intimacy that cannot be satisfied. H.'s passion, instead of connecting him to
others, is a form of confinement and separation. The conversations in the first section of *Liber Amoris* are displays of
a terrible awkwardness, of one person refusing to respond
to another. H.'s words and gestures are misunderstood, as
if hovering above a set of emotional needs and antagonisms
that can scarcely be expressed. H.'s efforts at apology
and reparation are fruitless. Love turns into its apparent
opposite – aggression – and then into guilty attempts to
repair the damage that comes from anger. H. wants his
beloved to be the source of a new happiness. Instead she
becomes his antagonist. He believes that she can promise him pleasure like no other. Her power to refuse
what she promises makes her all the more perplexing and
fearful.

The book's subtitle – 'The New Pygmalion' – suggests
that this solitude is not being displayed simply to evoke the

reader's pity. The title carries more than one echo from Rousseau. Where he had written a new and bestselling version of the story of the medieval lovers, Eloise and Abelard, Hazlitt attempted to do the same thing for an even older love story, Pygmalion. The Greek myth told the story of a sculptor, Pygmalion, who fell in love with one of his own creations, a statue of Galatea. Venus, the goddess of love, took pity on him and granted his wish that his statue be changed from stone to living flesh. In one version of the old story, Galatea returned the love of the man who had created her. Hazlitt set his version of the story in modern Britain. His Pygmalion is a writer, not a sculptor. His Galatea is not a statue in a sculptor's workshop but the daughter of a London lodging-house keeper.

His new Pygamalion is thus an ironic reversal of the old story. It tells of a passion that turns its object from flesh into stone. No benign goddess of love hovers over H.'s passion. He becomes a case study of a literary and self-conscious mind seeking to elicit another's love by the power of his words and imagination. But H.'s words do the opposite of what he intends. They harden S. against him. She refuses to be his invention.

Hazlitt interpreted his experience through literary comparisons and quotations. If these could lead him to think of his life as a tragedy, the example of the 'New Pygmalion' suggests another direction, one that led him towards an ironic understanding of what Sarah Walker had accused him of in one of their conversations: 'You sit and fancy things out of your own head, and then lay them to my charge.' A fitful enlightenment emerges in the book. Hazlitt had discerned the part his own imagination played in creating his own suffering. In this sense the book is about the costs of self-absorption. Idolising Sarah, Hazlitt cannot see her or understand her.

Liber Amoris is a book about illusions, about the way that love makes us see things that aren't there, and not see things that are. Hazlitt was certainly not alone in linking love to illusion. Rousseau had come to a similar conclusion about love in *La Nouvelle Heloise*. Its hero and heroine, Saint Preux and Julie, both acknowledge this, and Julie puts it into words:

> How attractive are love's illusions! These flatteries are in one sense true; judgment falls silent, but the heart speaks. The lover who praises us for perfections we don't have sees them just as he represents them to himself; he doesn't in the least bit lie while telling lies.

Love is always based on an exaggeration of the qualities of the beloved. But the lover believes in the truth of these exaggerations. They give us a glimpse of an ideal life; they produce intensities of feeling that are compelling motives for action.

If Hazlitt's book acknowledges Rousseau's perspective, it also echoes another eighteenth-century bestseller, Richardson's *Clarissa*. Like Richardson's book, Hazlitt's story hinges on a woman's determined refusal of a man's advances. H. shares with Richardson's demonic hero, Lovelace, a tendency to imagine his predicament through quotations from *Othello*, and *Liber Amoris* shares a crucial setting with Clarissa, a lodging house. But, however much it echoes previous stories, *Liber Amoris* does not simply imitate them. The story it tells us has a muted ending. S. does not die as Clarissa does, nor is H. killed in a duel like Lovelace. The reader may know that H. has died as a result of his fatal attachment, but his death is not a spectacular suicide, like Werther's. The book has a strange realism: love happens; it fails; life moves on.

In an essay published in March 1823, *On Dreams,* Hazlitt, without making the connection to *Liber Amoris* explicit, gave a remarkable commentary on the psychological state that is at the centre of the book. He reflected on the possibility that dreams give us a clue to our most powerful and involuntary feelings. If it is true that in dreams 'the curb is taken off our passions and our imagination wanders at will', then an odd consequence follows for Hazlitt's analysis of his emotional life:

It should appear that I have never been in love... I never dream of the face of anyone I am particularly attached to. I have thought almost to agony of the same person for years, nearly without ceasing so far as to have her face always before me and to be haunted by a perpetual consciousness of disappointed passion, and yet I never in all that time dreamt of this person more than once or twice, and then not vividly. I conceive therefore that this perseverance of imagination in a fruitless track must have been owing to mortified pride, to an intense desire and hope for good in the abstract, more than to love which I consider as an individual and involuntary passion, and in which therefore, when it is strong must predominate over the fancy in sleep... I think myself into love and dream myself out of it.

Hazlitt's passion, like the work of the modern

Pygmalion, is an invention. The analysis of illusion is taken a step further. Not just the beloved but love itself is willed into being, and not out of any attraction for a particular person, but from other motives: a compensation for hurt pride, an abstract longing for something good. From this perspective the *Liber Amoris* is not a love story, but a story about love's absence and the need that this creates in H. to convince himself that he is indeed in love. Yet that may be part of the book's subtlety, part of its disturbing account, because how, after all, except with hindsight, can the line be drawn between a love that comes unbidden and one that is sustained by the will? In *On Dreams* Hazlitt ruefully and wittily claims to know the difference, but the knowledge is precarious.

Liber Amoris, like *On Dreams*, is a work of self-analysis based on moments of confession and embarrassing revelation. The character of H. is not simply a thinly disguised version of Hazlitt. He is more like an earlier version of a self, someone whose psychological condition Hazlitt now wants to diagnose and leave behind. As before, writing about his life enabled Hazlitt to think about himself as if he were another person. The book may seem to confirm his argument that writers and love don't mix, but the new Pygmalion shows a capacity that doesn't apply to writers alone: to create illusions, and then become miserable by testing their truth.

Most contemporary reviewers of the book saw none of this subtlety. Some praised it. The *Times* reviewer found it morally instructive as an 'able delineation' of a man under the influence of a 'degrading infatuation'. Another, writing in the *Globe*, claimed the book was 'unique in the English language', compared it to Rousseau, and thought it 'most courageously told'. But far more column inches were devoted to destroying the book than defending it. If Hazlitt had intended to defy his most vitriolic critics in publishing *Liber Amoris*, he could scarcely have anticipated the scale of the hostility it provoked.

Within a week of its publication the *Monthly Literary Register* attacked the book. Its review made clear that any effort by Hazlitt to disguise the origins of *Liber Amoris* in his own life had failed. Hazlitt was identified as its author and taken as an example of 'these liberal and radical rapscallions, who take upon them the airs of philosophers, poets, disseminators of truth, improvers of taste, reformers of abuses, and ameliators (sic) of mankind, as they call themselves'.

What the book inadvertently did was reveal the real character of radicalism in all its immorality and 'slavering sensuality'. Sarah Walker did not escape censure either. The reviewer identified 'S.' as the daughter of Hazlitt's landlord and went on to denounce her as 'an artful, shameless, trumpery, common strumpet'. Hazlitt's passion was a ludicrous mistake, a mixing-up of things that should be kept separate. No landlord's daughter could be the object of a refined love. Hazlitt had been finding value where there was none.

The number of attacks increased in the weeks that followed. Some of these played off each other. On May 31st, a reviewer for the *Museum* pretended to doubt that the book could be by Hazlitt. He might be 'a vain and weak man whose principles are at war with the best feelings of society', but he had some intelligence and *Liber Amoris*, a 'disgusting mass of profligacy and dullness', could only have been written by 'the veriest dunce of literature'.

It was through the columns of *John Bull*, the sister publication of the *Monthly Literary Register*, that Hazlitt was to discover exactly how much his enemies knew about his passion for Sarah Walker. In its June 15th issue, the paper announced that it would take a 'double view' of the book and its author. It would first invite its readers to laugh at 'this cockney's stupidity and folly'. It would then instruct them to 'shrink with disgust' from the spectacle of

Hazlitt's behaviour. Unlike its sister publication, *John Bull*'s reviewer decided to defend Sarah's character:

We say why should this young woman be calumniated? Why should this disappointed dotard – the impotent sensualist – gratify the only passion he has in his power to enjoy, SPITE, at the expense of a young woman.

The following Sunday the paper continued its denunciation. In addition to its 'double view', it offered an exposé: the whole truth of the story behind *Liber Amoris* could now be told. As far as *John Bull* was concerned, Hazlitt's editing of his letters could not be in the service of art. It was just a crude attempt to conceal the extent of his folly.

Towards the end of the book, Hazlitt had included an edited version of a letter he had sent to Sarah from Scotland in March 1822. *John Bull* published the whole text of the letter, full of endearments and affectionate banter. They justified their action by claiming that they had simply followed where Hazlitt had led: '...if he feels offended or sore that his private letters are thus made public, he must reconcile himself by recollecting that it is he himself who has given publicity to the affair altogether.' As far as the paper was concerned, the letter showed all the foolishness of a middle-aged married man trying to woo a younger woman. With the letter published, *John Bull* decided 'we are quite done with Mr. Hazlitt.'

How the newspaper got hold of the letter is not clear. Sarah Walker may have given or sold it to one of their journalists. It may have been stolen from Southampton Buildings by one of the lodgers and passed on to the newspaper. What its publication confirmed is how close Hazlitt's enemies could get to his private life. He was a man who was under close surveillance.

Hazlitt made no attempt to respond to these attacks or to find out how one of his love letters had finished up in the hands of his enemies. The hostile reviews had killed *Liber Amoris*'s chances of commercial success. No further edition of it appeared in Hazlitt's life time. Thereafter the book had a fitful existence. In 1839 Douglas Jerrold published a parody of *Liber Amoris*, called *The Metaphysician and the Maid*. In 1894 the decadent poet, Richard le Galliene, published *Liber Amoris* in a limited edition. By this time it had a reputation as a pornographic and scandalous book.

In the twentieth century, *Liber Amoris* survived in scholarly editions of Hazlitt's work and in paperback editions that fitfully go in and out of print. Certainly the book retains its power to disturb its readers. It is judged to be misogynistic — the story of a middle-aged man's frantic attempts to manipulate a young woman into marriage — or nihilistic, a book that seems to drain any sense of value out of the world it presents. Some Hazlitt scholars see the book as a one-off, something that is at once wholly typical of its author but unconnected to the rest of his work.

Yet all these judgements seem to miss something about the book's texture and tone. The story is as much about the power of a woman's refusal as it is about an attempted seduction. By the end of the story H. has accepted that S. has defeated him, that however powerful his passion might seem to him, it has only a very limited effect upon her. And this is connected to one of the book's most powerful and oddly contemporary themes, the interplay between language and feeling, between experiencing an emotion and finding a way of persuasively expressing it. Each of the sections of the book displays this theme in a different stage of development. In the first H. seeks to initiate and sustain his love for S.; in the second he writes about the emotional crisis this provokes in his letters to his friend, C.P.; in the third he retells the story of his passion from the perspective of its failure, this time in the long letter to J.S.K. In each we see him seeking out a language that will sustain his passion or analyse it or console him for its consequences. *Liber Amoris* is a story about love's failure, told with that commitment to honesty that Hazlitt's contemporaries found both admirable and disturbing

After so many words written and spoken about his passion for Sarah Walker, Hazlitt became virtually silent about the affair. A letter written in July 1823 to Thomas Hood, an assistant editor of the *London Magazine*, gave a hint about the reasons for his silence. Hazlitt wanted to explain why there had been some delay in continuing his series of essays on the picture galleries of England. He used a phrase that echoed some words used in an earlier letter to Thomas Noon Talfourd about the impact of Sarah on his life: 'something happened which hurt my mind'. This 'something' may be the attacks on *Liber Amoris* rather than Sarah's behaviour towards him. But Hazlitt indicated another cause, one that connects his sense of the effects of his words upon himself and others with his belief that Sarah might be one of his readers:

I used to think she saw and perhaps approved these articles: but whatever I can do, implying an idea of taste and elegance, only makes me more odious to myself, and tantalises me with feelings which I can

never hope to excite in others — wretch that I am,
and am to be, till I am nothing!

Knowing that, despite his hopes, his words could not
win Sarah's approval made him seem a fool to himself. The
feelings that art provoked in him could not be shared with
her. To escape this torment Hazlitt would need to rid himself of the desire that she might read his work and, in reading him, come to love him. Silence about her seemed the
best way to achieve this end. According to Haydon he
spent a couple of nights in September renewing his vigil of
Southampton Buildings. But his obsession with Sarah was
fading. She ceased to dominate his imagination and his
hopes for a new life.

EPILOGUE

Sarah Walker gave birth to a son, Frederick, some time between March and October 1824. She had moved out of Southampton Buildings and her child was born in Somers Town near St. Pancras. This is where her grandmother had lived and, although she had died in February 1823, it's possible that Sarah had decided to stay in her house. Soon after the birth of her son she began to live with John Tomkins, the child's father, although there is no record of a marriage. Sarah took Tomkins' name and lived with him for more than twenty years. He became a qualified solicitor and by 1841 the couple were living together at 31 Gloucester Street, not far from Southampton Buildings.

Then something went wrong. Tomkins lost his status as

a lawyer and had to take on work as a clerk. By 1851 the couple were no longer living together and Sarah moved in with her son Frederick and his wife. Alcohol may have been the cause of their separation. When he died in 1858 one of the causes of John Tomkins' death was erysipelas, a skin inflammation associated with heavy drinking.

By 1850 Sarah had become a grandmother and by 1852 she had moved with her son and family to the prosperous suburb of Highgate. But in the same year her son died at the age of 28 from cerebral dropsy. After Sarah's daughter-in-law remarried, the family moved south of the Thames to Newington, where Sarah continued to live with them until 1871, when she moved into a lodging house not far from Newington Crescent. She died there in 1878 at the age of 77. Her younger brother Miciah, who had enjoyed bawdy jokes about the lodgers in Southampton Buildings, became a successful lawyer. In a family memoir he wrote in 1882, he stated that his sister had died as a spinster. For the respectable lawyer Miciah there was something unseemly about his sister's life. He did not want its truth remembered.

As for Hazlitt, in August 1824, Mary Shelley met him after a break of six years and was shocked by his appearance: '... gaunt and thin, his hair scattered, his cheek bones projecting... his smile brought tears into my eyes, it was like a sun-beam illuminating the most melancholy ruins'. It's easy to imagine that Hazlitt's appearance bore witness to his rejection by Sarah, but the truth was a little different. In the same year that Mary Shelley saw him he married Isabella Bridgewater, a well-to-do widow. What he had talked about with his first wife Sarah after their divorce had come true. He had found a woman whose money he hoped would stave off financial insecurity. The new husband and wife travelled together in France and Italy, and during their stay in Paris Hazlitt met Stendhal, another writer who sympathised with Napoleon and had published *De l'amour*, another study on passion, a year before *Liber Amoris* came out.

Hazlitt continued to publish prolifically in Paris and London. One of his most famous works, *The Spirit of the Age*, came out in 1825. The following year saw the publication of another collection of essays, *The Plain Speaker*, and his *Notes of a Journey through France and Italy*.

Then, in 1827, his marriage to Isabella ended. Why this happened is not certain, but it is likely that financial disagreements had a lot to do with it. Isabella expected Hazlitt to earn money as a writer. He expected her to support him while he dedicated himself to the research and writing of his life of Napoleon. Hazlitt's son, William, stayed with the couple in Paris in the late summer of 1826 and there seemed to be an expectation that Isabella would help support him as well. Perhaps she couldn't tolerate the 'women of the town'. By the autumn of 1827, the couple had separated.

Sarah Hazlitt, continued to follow her husband's career. She was in Paris in 1824 and clearly knew about his plans. He continued to give her money. By 1827 it is possible that they were living in the same house together at Winterslow. It was certainly a place Hazlitt continued to visit. In 1828 he wrote a letter from there complaining about the postal service.

From 1827 Hazlitt suffered increasingly from ill-health. He continued to publish essays and reviews and volumes of his biography of Napoleon. Away from Winterslow, he moved from one London address to another. By 1830 he was living in Frith Street, Soho, and it was here that he died, probably from stomach cancer, on the afternoon of September 18th. His oldest friend, Charles Lamb, was with him and so was his son, one of his publishers, James Hessey, and another friend, Edmund White.

Money remained a problem right up until the end. Hazlitt's last letter was written to his favourite editor,

Murray, a few days before his death:

Dear Sir,
I am dying. Can you send me £10 and so consummate your many kindnesses to me.

In the event, Murray sent him £50 with characteristic generosity.

Something else persisted as well. Some of his friends were convinced that in the last years of his life Hazlitt had developed a special relationship with 'one of the girls of the Theatre'. In his own way, and despite his self-knowledge, Hazlitt continued to imagine himself in love.

ACKNOWLEDGMENTS

My greatest debt is to Richard Holmes who has been an unfailing source of encouragement, advice and thoughtful criticism. I'm also grateful to the following for varied but always helpful comments, some of them at the last minute: John Barnard, Gillian and John Beer, Denise Riley, William St. Clair, Katri Skala, and Duncan Wu. I have benefited from the work of many Hazlitt scholars and biographers, especially A.C. Grayling, the late Stanley Jones, and Charles Nicholls for his work on the later life of Sarah Walker.

This work is based, wherever possible, on primary sources. Thanks to the staff of the Special Collection at the University of Buffalo Library, the British Library, and the Cambridge University Library. Thanks also to the University of East Anglia for providing the research leave that enabled me to complete this book.

I owe more than thanks to Alice Tomkins, and to Diane DeBell who took time to read an earlier version of this book and discuss it with me.

References

Hazlitt's work is available in a variety of editions and selections. References to the *Liber Amoris* come from the Gotham Library edition, edited by Gerald Lahey, and published by New York University Press in 1980. References to Hazlitt's letters come from *The Letters of William Hazlitt*, edited by Sykes, Bonner and Lahey, New York University Press, 1978. This is also the edition that contains Hazlitt's journal for March 4th–16th 1823. Quotations from Sarah Hazlitt's journals come from *The Journals of William and Sarah Hazlitt*, edited by W.H. Bonner, University of Buffalo, 1959. Unless otherwise stated, references to Hazlitt's essays are taken from P.P. Howe's edition of his *Collected Works*, J.M. Dent and Sons, London, 1930

Page 16: '... the first time...', *Liber Amoris*, p 87
Page 16: 'silent and motionless...', P.G. Patmore, *My Friends and Acquaintances*, Saunders and Otley, London, 1854, p 250
Page 16: 'a silent picture...throwing under gazes', John Clare, *John Clare by Himself*, Carcanet Press, Manchester, 1996
Page 17: 'Her face was...', B.W. Procter, *An Autobiographical*

Fragment, edited by Coventry Patmore, 1877, pp181-2

Page 18: '...you come up here...', *Liber Amoris*, p 86

Page 19: 'I do not think...', *On The Knowledge of Character*, *Collected Works*, VOL. VIII, pp 310-11

Page 20: '...it was the excess...', *Conversations of James Northcote Esq RA* in *Collected Works*, Volume XI, p 278.

Page 21: '...however she might agree...', *Liber Amoris*, p 152

Page 24: 'I started in life...', *On The Feeling of Immortality in Youth*, *Hazlitt*, *Selected Essays*, edited by Geoffrey Keynes, The Nonesuch Press, London, 1970, p 317 and cf. Howe, *Collected Works*, VOL. XVII, p 196

Page 25: 'Men are born free...', *Declaration of the Rights of Man*, 1789 (http://www.yale.edu/lawweb/avalon/rightsof.htm)

Page 27: 'wild black-bill Hazlitt...', 'Hazlitt Cross-Questioned', *Blackwood's*, August 1818, pp 550-52

Page 28: 'ludicrous egotism', 'Political Essays', *Quarterly Review*, November 1819, pp 158-63

Page 29: 'class of writers...', 'Hazlitt's Essays, Criticisms and Lectures', *British Review*, May 1819, pp 313-39

Page 29: 'Cockney Aristotle..', 'On The Cockney School of Poetry. No V', *Blackwood's*, April 1819, pp 97-100

Page 29: 'scatter the seeds...', 'On The Cockney School of Prose Writers. No 11. Hazlitt's Lectures', *New Monthly*

Magazine, November 1818, pp 299-304

Page 31: 'It appears that Hazlitt…', *Henry Crabb Robinson on Books and Their Writers*, edited by E.J. Morley, Dent, London, 1938, p 169. The Latin phrase *more puerorum* means 'in the manner of boys'.

Page 31: 'addicted to women…', *Unpublished Letters of Samuel Taylor Coleridge*, edited by E.L. Griggs, Constable, London, 1932, p 279

Page 32: 'Like other gross sensualists…', *Crabb Robinson on Books and Their Writers*, p 6

Page 32: 'The scapes of the great god…', *The Letters of Charles and Mary Lamb*, edited by E.W. Marris, Cornell University Press, Ithaca and London, 1978, VOL. III, p 125

Page 33: 'Introduce him to a tea-party of…', *On The Conversation of Authors* in *Collected Works*, VOL. XII, p 125

Page 33: 'real persons and things', *On The Literary Character*, *Collected Works*, VOL. IV, p 133

Page 34: 'the blow…', *On The Literary Character* in *Collected Works*, VOL. IV, p 135

Page 34: 'living death… when it returns…', *On The Literary Character* in *Collected Works*, pp 135-136

Page 37: 'I am now down…', *Letters*, p 202

Page 38: 'the little Nero', *The Letters of John Keats*, edited by H.E. Rollins, VOL. II, Cambridge University Press,

Cambridge, 1958, p 59

Page 39: 'a troublesome...', *Crabb Robinson on Books and Their Writers*, p 265

Page 40: 'in her morning gown...', *Letters*, p 249 and *Liber Amoris*, p 129

Page 40: 'The love of a man like Petrarch...', *Sismondi's, Literature of the South* in *CollectedWorks* VOL. XVI, p 45

Page 42: '...upwards of £30 worth...', *Liber Amoris*, unpublished manuscript, University of Buffalo

Page 43: 'three volumes of my own writings...' unpublished manuscript and cf. *Liber Amoris*, p 216

Page 45: 'an incarnate fiend', *My Friends and Acquaintances*, p 260

Page 46: 'Here however...', *My Friends and Acquaintances*, p 276

Page 47: 'His forbearance...', *My Friends and Acquaintances,* p 276

Page 48: 'I was never in a...', *On Living to Oneself* in *Collected Works*, VOL. VIII, p 90

Page 49: 'He who looks...', *On Living to Oneself* in *Collected Works*, VOL. VIII, pp 95-96

Page 50: 'With what a wavering air...', *On Living to Oneself* in *CollectedWorks*, VOL. VIII, p 96

Page 50: '…defend me from meeting…', *On Living to Oneself* in *Collected Works*, VOL. VIII, p 96

Page 51: 'Sir, Doctor Read…', in Stanley Jones, *Hazlitt: A Life*, Clarendon Press, Oxford, 1989, pp 316-7

Page 52: 'Without that pale face…', *The Past and the Future, in Collected Works*, VOL. VIII, p 24. Keats's *La Belle Dame Sans Merci* was first published in Leigh Hunt's Journal, the *Indicator*, in May 1820. The same issue has a bearing on Hazlitt's *Liber Amoris*. Hunt published a translation of Rousseau's verse play, *Pygmalion*. Hazlitt was to subtitle *Liber Amoris*, *The New Pygmalion*. In his preface to Keats's poem Hunt condemns the modern worship of 'Mammon' and argues that the sufferings that come from 'the worship of Love exalt and humanise us, and those from the worship of Mammon debase and brutalise'. Perhaps Hazlitt was testing the exalting and humanising powers of love in his passion for Sarah Walker and in *Liber Amoris*.

Page 54: 'Pride of birth', *Liber Amoris*, p 80

Page 58: 'depth of taste…', *The Letters of John Keats*, VOL. I, p 203

Page 59: 'unwashed, unshaved…', *The Autobiography of Benjamin Robert Haydon,* edited by Edmund Blunden, Oxford University Press, Oxford, 1927, p 283

Page 59: 'But I thought of him…, *On Coffee House Politicians* in *Collected Works*, VOL. VIII, p 196

Page 61: 'man of undoubted…', 'Table Talk by Mr. Hazlitt', *London Magazine*, April 1821, p 431

Page 61: 'They do not merely guide us…', 'Hazlitt's Table Talk', *London Magazine*, May 1821, pp 545-50

Page 62: 'vilest indelicacy…', 'Table Talk', *New Edinburgh Review,* July 1821, pp 100-21

Page 62: 'him out of his envelope…', 'Table Talk', *British Critic*, June 1821, pp 629-34

Page 62: 'crude though belaboured… insane extravagance… Slang-whanger… one who makes use of…', 'Table Talk', *Quarterly Review*, October 1821, pp 103-8

Page 63: 'philosophical fanatic… fire in his eye…', *On Paradox or Commonplace* in *Collected Works*, VOL. VIII, p 148

Page 64: 'You provoke me into thinking…', *Letters*, p 204

Page 65: 'brother-reformers…', in A.C. Grayling, *The Quarrel of the Age*, Phoenix Press, London, 2000, p 266

Page 65: 'irrepressible love…', *The Quarrel of the Age*, p 267

Page 66: 'I have no faith in…', *The Quarrel of the Age*, p 267

Page 66: 'If I have teased…', *The Quarrel of the Age*, p 267

Page 67: 'but indifferent…' *Letters*, p 208

Page 67: 'alter it or…', *Letters*, p 208

Page 69: 'felt no interest… cost him… so annoyed and

cramped...', *The Quarrel of the Age,* p 270

Page 71: 'The instant...', *Letters*, p 278-9 and cf. *Liber Amoris* p 162

Page 72: 'despised looks...', *Liber Amoris*, p 241

Page 73: 'Betsey: Oh! If those trousers...', *Letters*, p 270

Page 75: 'You sit and fancy things...', *Liber Amoris*, p 91

Page 77: 'The truth is...' Hazlitt, *Letters*, p212

Page 77: 'Life is a continued struggle...', *Lectures on the Age of Elizabeth*, *Collected Works,* VOL. VI, p 364

Page 77: 'My dear Talfourd...', *Letters*, p 212

Page 78: 'I argued...', *The Fight*, Howe, *Collected Works*, VOL. XVII, p 74

Page 79: 'wrapped in... keep off...', *The Fight* in *Collected Works*, VOL. XVII, p 74

Page 79: 'putting the will...', *The Fight* in *Collected Works*, VOL. XVII, p 74

Page 79: 'in high spirits', *The Fight* in *Collected Works*, VOL. XVII, p 86

Page 80: 'Besides I had better Spirits...', Stewart C. Wilcox, *Hazlitt in the Workshop*, The John Hopkins Press, Baltimore, 1943, p 48

Page 80: 'for eight and forty hours...', *My Friends and Acquaintances*, p 280

Page 84: 'Oh! my sitting down...' *Letters,* p 243 and

cf. *Liber Amoris,* p 107

Page 85: 'agony of the moment...', *Liber Amoris*, p 96

Page 85: 'tradesman's daughter', *Liber Amoris*, p 99

Page 87: 'On the road down...', *Letters* p 246 and cf. *Liber Amoris*, pp 116-7

Page 90: 'You will scold me...', *Letters* p 214 and cf. *Liber Amoris,* p 103

Page 91: 'You once made me...', *Letters* pp 214-5 and cf. *Liber Amoris,* p 104

Page 91: 'I thought to have...', *Letters*, p 215 and cf. *Liber Amoris,* p 104

Page 93: 'All your fine sentiments...', *Letters,* p 231

Page 94: 'pretensions... dress and address', *Letters,* p 231, 233

Page 95: 'a spider, my dear...', *Letters,* p 235

Page 96: 'rapidity of his transition... the conflicts of passion', *Mr. Kean's Shylock* in *Collected Works*, VOL. V, p 179

Page 96: 'mouth greatly resembled...', *My Friends and Acquaintances* , p 283.

Page 97: 'little Yes and No... arrant jilt', *Letters*, p 239 and cf. *Liber Amoris*, p 118

Page 97: 'Could you not come and...', *Letters*, p 240 and cf. *Liber Amoris,* p 120

Page 98: 'You are such a girl... unkind word... That delicious night', *Letters,* pp 241-2 and cf. *Liber Amoris*, p 107

Page 98: 'Can I ever forget…', *Letters*, p 203 and cf. *Liber Amoris*, p 107

Page 99: 'bad passions… good feelings', *Letters*, p 244

Page 101: 'dull and out of spirits', *Letters*, p 248

Page 102: 'Can you account for it…' *Letters,* p 247 and cf. *Liber Amoris,* p 122

Page 102: 'To be hated, loathed…', *Letters*, p 247

Page 102: 'to be an ideot…,' *Letters,* p 248 and cf. *Liber Amoris,* p 123

Page 103: 'that gentle form…', *On The Knowledge of Character* in *Collected Works*, VOL. VIII, p 311

Page 104: 'The greatest hypocrite…', *On The Knowledge of Character* in *Collected Works*, VOL. VIII, p 305

Page 105: 'What security can I have…', *Letters,* p 249

Page 105: 'FINAL. Don't got at all…', *Letters,* p 251

Page 106: 'All she wants…', *Letters,* p 251

Page 107: '… it is so she has oftenest…', *Letters,* p 249 and cf. *Liber Amoris,* p 129.

Page 107: 'I went with a girl…', *Letters*, p 249

Page 109: 'he had done a most injudicious thing…', *The Journals of William and Sarah Hazlitt*, p 248

Page 110: 'But shouldst thou…', *On Great and Little Things* in *Collected Works*, VOL. VIII, pp 235-6

Page 111: 'I beg the reader to consider…', *On Great and Little*

Things in *Collected Works*, VOL. VIII, p 235

Page 112: 'common lodging-house drab', *Letters,* p 251

Page 112: 'To lip a wanton...', William Shakespeare, *Othello*, Act IV, scene 1, ll. 73-4

Page 112: 'She is my soul's idol...', *Letters,* p 254 cf. *Liber Amoris*, p 125

Page 113: 'When I sometimes think...', *Letters,* p 255 cf. *Liber Amoris,* p 127

Page 115: 'deficient in those minutiae...', quoted in Stanley Jones, *Hazlitt: A Life*, Oxford University Press, 1989, p 11

Page 117: 'the City of London... had carnal and adulterous intercourse', *The Journals of William and Sarah Hazlitt,* p 190

Page 119: 'in a state...', *The Journals of William and Sarah Hazlitt,* p 188

Page 121: 'handsome present... to love money', *The Journals of William and Sarah Hazlitt,* p195

Page 121: 'went picking up girls...', *The Journals of William and Sarah Hazlitt,* p196

Page 122: 'Nobody was more sore...', *The Journals of William and Sarah Hazlitt,* p196

Page 122: '... if he entered a coffee house...', *My Friends and Acquaintances*, p 350

Page 125: 'The air thickened...', *Liber Amoris,* p 196

Page 127: 'I see you brought me back...', *Liber Amoris,* pp 199-200

Page 129: 'I could not stay...', *Liber Amoris,* p 206

Page 129: 'the desolation...', *Liber Amoris,* p 207

Page 130: 'with no friendly aspect', *Liber Amoris,* p 208

Page 130: 'an accident...', *Liber Amoris,* p 210

Page 131: 'Pieces of a broken heart...', *Liber Amoris,* p 214

Page 132: 'childish, wanton... I murmured her name...', *Liber Amoris,* p 218

Page 133: 'guilty of improprieties...', *LiberAmoris,* p 222

Page 133: 'light creature', *Liber Amoris,* p 222

Page 133: 'keep every lodger...', *Liber Amoris,* p 223

Page 134: 'I started to find...', *Liber Amoris,* p 229

Page 134: 'smiling with smothered delight...', *Liber Amoris,* p 230

Page 135: 'withered, cadaverous...', *Liber Amoris,* p 230

Page 135: 'I always told you...', *Letters,* pp 261, 263 cf. *Liber Amoris,* p 133

Page 135: 'I was driven from her presence...', *Letters,* p 261 cf. *Liber Amoris,* p133

Page 135: 'The people about me...', *Liber Amoris,* p 261 cf. *Liber Amoris,* p 134

Page 135: 'hardened, impudent...', *Letters,* p 263

Page 135: 'She has an itch...', *Letters,* p 263

Page 136: 'The bitch wants a stallion...', *Letters*, p 264

Page 136: 'Yet if only I knew...', *Letters*, p 265

Page 138: 'were such low, vulgar...', *The Journals of William and Sarah Hazlitt*, p 210

Page 139: 'very nervous and poorly...', *The Journals of William and Sarah Hazlitt*, p 210

Page 139: 'very high wind...', *The Journals of William and Sarah Hazlitt*, p 210

Page 139: 'Mrs. Knight at the window...', *The Journals of William and Sarah Hazlitt*, p 213

Page 140: 'My dear little baby...', *Letters*, p 262

Page 141: 'being overcome... cut through...', *The Journals of William and Sarah Hazlitt*, p 221

Page 143: 'unfit for any...', *The Journals of William and Sarah Hazlitt*, p 225

Page 144: 'In the evening...', *The Journals of William and Sarah Hazlitt*, p 225

Page 146: 'Instead of that delicious...', *Letters*, p 267 and cf. *Liber Amoris*, p 142

Page 147: 'Can there be a doubt...', *Letters*, p 270

Page 149: 'she had been frightened into...', *The Journals of William and Sarah Hazlitt*, p 226

Page 149: 'I was so nervous...', *The Journals of William and Sarah Hazlitt*, p 227

Page 150: 'by the way', *The Journals of William and Sarah Hazlitt*, p 227

Page 150: 'he pulled...', *The Journals of William and Sarah Hazlitt*, p 228

Page 151: 'Walked to the Glasgow...', *The Journals of William and Sarah Hazlitt*, p 228

Page 153: 'She was my life...', *Letters*, p 274 and cf. *Liber Amoris*, p 136

Page 154: 'still to be won...', *Liber Amoris*, p 177

Page 155: 'drove me mad', *Letters*, p 286 and cf. *Liber Amoris*, p 182

Page 155: 'he thought that...', *The Journals of William and Sarah Hazlitt*, pp 246-7

Page 156: 'he was only sorry...', *The Journals of William and Sarah Hazlitt*, p 248

Page 157: 'good fortune... so that he might...', *The Journals of William and Sarah Hazlitt*, p 249

Page 157: 'He said that...', *The Journals of William and Sarah Hazlitt*, p 247

Page 157: 'improper or indelicate', *The Journals of William and Sarah Hazlitt*, p 247

Page 158: 'it had often struck him...', *The Journals of William and Sarah Hazlitt*, p 247

Page 158: 'on my forehead alone...', *Letters*, p 289

Page 159: 'If she will...', *Letters*, p 289

Page 159: 'It is all over...', *Letters*, p 290

Page 162: 'She still absented...', *Liber Amoris*, p 232

Page 163: 'so she stood...', *Liber Amoris*, p 234

Page 164: 'There is hardly...', *On Gusto* in *Collected Works*, VOL. IV, p 77

Page 167: 'I took nearly...', *Liber Amoris*, p 236

Page 167: 'the whole of the next morning...', *Liber Amoris*, p 236

Page 168: 'Something... withheld me', *Liber Amoris*, p 238

Page 169: 'sitting in the window seat...', *Liber Amoris*, p 238

Page 169: 'tall, rather well-looking...', *Liber Amoris*, p 239

Page 170: 'felt deep grief...', *Liber Amoris*, p 242

Page 172: 'I am no more lifted...', *Liber Amoris*, p 247

Page 173: 'a more complete experiment...', *Liber Amoris*, p 248

Page 174: 'It is one faultless...', *Liber Amoris*, p 251

Page 175: 'I had embraced the false...', *Liber Amoris*, p 246

Page 175: 'like a weed', *Liber Amoris*, p 256

Page 176: 'I have since I returned...', *Letters*, p 291

Page 176: 'Hazlitt called...', *The Diary of Benjamin Robert Haydon*, edited by W.B. Pope, Harvard University Press, Cambridge, Mass., 1960, VOL. II, pp 375-6

Page 177: 'Down he goes...', *The Diary of Benjamin Robert*

Haydon, p 374

Page 178: 'I am a cursed fool...', *An Autobiographical Fragment*, pp 180-1

Page 179: 'let us have no more...', 'Hazlitt's Table Talk', *Monthly Literary Register*, August 1822, pp 52-60

Page 181: 'old, hard, weather-beaten... Since this affair...' *Haydon, Correspondence and Table Talk*, edited by F.W. Haydon, Chatto and Windus, London, 1876, VOL. II, p 76

Page 181: 'He has written down...', *Haydon, Correspondence and Table Talk*, p 75

Page 183: 'I hated the sight of myself...', *Letters*, p 322

Page 185: 'All we want is to...', *On The Spirit of Monarchy* in *Collected Works*, VOL. XIX, p 255

Page 186: 'Somehow that period...', *My First Acquaintance* in *Collected Works*, VOL. XVII, p 116

Page 187: 'So I have loitered..', *My First Acquaintance* in *Collected Works*, VOL. XVII, p 116

Page 188: 'a troop of yahoos', *On the Scotch Character* in *Collected Works*, VOL. XVII, p 106

Page 188: 'savage system...', *On The Periodical Press* in *Collected Works*, VOL. XVI, p239

Page 188: 'the extent and extravagance of the abuse...', *On The Periodical Press* in *Collected Works*, VOL. XVI, p 239

Page 190: 'kissed her several times…', *Letters*, p 381

Page 190: 'his hand upon her thigh…', *Letters*, p 386

Page 191: 'F. got between…', *Letters*, p 387

Page 191: 'Saturday March 15th…', *Letters*, p 388

Page 191: 'seen in close conference… what divine music…', *Letters*, p 381

Page 192: 'little ideot', *Letters*, p 385

Page 192: 'determined to keep…', *Letters*, p 381

Page 192: 'Decoy! Damned…', *Letters*, p 383

Page 193: 'disappointment…', *Liber Amoris*, p 63

Page 194: 'fatal attachment', *Liber Amoris*, p 63

Page 194: 'his strongest feeling…', *Liber Amoris*, p 64

Page 199: 'How attractive…', *La Nouvelle Heloise Oeuvres* in *Completes de J-J Rousseau,* edited by B. Gagnebin & Marcel Raymond, Pleiade Edition, Paris, 1959, VOL. XI, p 129 (translated by the author).

Page 201: 'the curb is taken off…', *On Dreams* in *Collected Works,* VOL. XII, p 23

Page 201: 'It should never appear…', *On Dreams* in *Collected Works,* VOL. XII, p 23

Page 203: 'able delineation…', '*Liber Amoris*', *The Times*, May 30th, 1823, p 3

Page 203 'unique in the English language… most courageously…', *the Globe,* May 1823

Page 203: 'these liberal and radical...' *'Liber Amoris'*, *Monthly Literary Register*, May 1823, pp 305-8, pp 322-25

Page 203: 'slavering sensuality... an artful, shameful...', as above

Page 204: 'a vain and weak man... disgusting mass... the veriest dunce', *'Liber Amoris'*, *Museum*, p 338-39

Page 204: 'a double view... this cockney's stupidity and folly... shrink with disgust', *'Liber Amoris'*, *John Bull*, June 15th, 1823

Page 205: 'We say why...', *'Liber Amoris'*, *John Bull*, June 15th, 1823, p 189

Page 205: 'if he feels offended or sore...', *John Bull,* June 22nd, 1823, pp 197-98

Page 206: 'we are quite done...', *John Bull,* June 22nd, 1823, p 198

Page 208: 'something happened...', *Letters*, p 328

Page 208: 'I used to think...', *Letters*, p 328

Page 214: 'Dear Sir, I am dying...', *Letters*, p 378

How to Be a Bad Birdwatcher
To the greater glory of life
Simon Barnes
1-904977-05-7 Paperback   £7.99

Look out of the window.

See a bird.

Enjoy it.

Congratulations. You are now a bad birdwatcher.

Anyone who has ever gazed up at the sky or stared out of
the window knows something about birds. In this funny,
inspiring, eye-opening book, Simon Barnes paints a rivet-
ing picture of how birdwatching has framed his life and can
help us all to a better understanding of our place on this
planet.

How to be a Bad Birdwatcher shows why birdwatching is
not the preserve of twitchers, but one of the simplest,
cheapest and most rewarding pastimes around.

"A delightful ode to the wild world outside
the kitchen window"
Daily Telegraph

The Good Granny Guide
Or how to be a modern grandmother
Jane Fearnley-Whittingstall
1-9040977-70-7 Paperback £8.99

In *The Good Granny Guide*, Jane Fearnley-Whittingstall provides a wonderfully entertaining insight into the joys − and pitfalls − of being a grandmother. A closely involved granny of five, she has gathered first-hand tips from other grandparents and their families in many different situations. The result is a vast resource of practical ideas to help you make the most of the time you spend with your grandchildren, plus invaluable advice on everything from childcare troubleshooting to what NOT to say to the daughter-in-law.

"Sound on everything from nappies to tantrums.
Jane Fearnley-Whittingstall gets the golden
rules right. She is spot on."
Philip Howard, *The Times*

Amo, amas, amat... and all that

How to become a Latin lover

Harry Mount

1-9040977-54-5 Hardback £12.99

Have you ever found yourself irritated when a *sine qua non* or a *mea culpa* is thrown into the conversation by a particularly annoying person? Or do distant memories of afternoons spent struggling to learn obscure verbs fill you with dread?

Never fear! (or as a Latin show-off might say, *Nil Desperandum!*) In this delightful guided tour of Latin, which features everything from a Monty Python grammar lesson to David Beckham's tattoos and all the best snippets of prose and poetry from 2000 years of literary history, Harry Mount wipes the dust off those boring primers and breathes life back into the greatest language of them all.

"Mount's love of Latin shines out on every page"

Spectator

"This breezy guide to the Latin language sugars the grammatical pill with well-placed jokes and friendly 'I'm on your side' advice." Mary Beard, *Daily Telegraph*

The Meaning of Sport

Simon Barnes

1-9040977-45-6 Hardback £16.99

In *The Meaning of Sport*, award-winning sports writer Simon Barnes gives you his grandstand seat for a journey from the Olympic Games in Athens to the World Cup in Germany – via the Ashes series, the Ryder Cup, Wimbledon, and more. He examines why sport holds us all in such thrall, how it uplifts and crushes us – and can seem to matter more than life itself. He challenges us to recognise the intelligence of Wayne Rooney, the making of Freddie Flintoff, the mythic nature of Steve Redgrave; and he ponders the ultimate cruelty of the game.

This is the book which asks the questions no one else has thought of, and finds some surprising answers. Sport has never been written about like this before.

"His book is a delight: full of wisdom, humour and whimsy and shows that, when done well, sports books can compete on any level." Michael Atherton